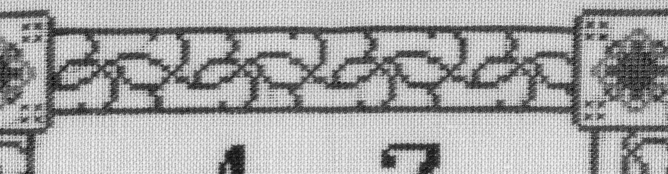

A to Z
CROSS-STITCH
SAMPLERS

The Vanessa-Ann Collection

To my brother "Peter Pan,"

With love from "Wendy"

Library of Congress Catalog Number: 88-064042
ISBN: 0-8487-0715-X
Manufactured in the United States of America
First Printing 1989

Executive Editor: Nancy J. Fitzpatrick
Production Manager: Jerry Higdon
Associate Production Manager: Rick Litton
Art Director: Bob Nance

A to Z Cross-Stitch Samplers

Editor: Linda Baltzell Wright
Copy Chief: Mary Jean Haddin
Photographers: Ryne Hazen;
cover by Colleen Duffley

The poems used for the introductions were written by Kristen Jarchow, Layton, Utah.

To find out how you can order *Cooking Light* magazine, write to *Cooking Light*®, P.O. Box C-549, Birmingham, AL 35283

CONTENTS

INTRODUCTION

This alphabet adventure is filled with samplers A to Z;
the search was far and wide to assure variety.
With linen, silk, and cotton, the ideas materialized into
colorful cross-stitch designs that are very personalized.

The artists sometimes say that they reflect their very soul;
in pouring out their hopes and joys, their samplers become whole.
Adorned with names and dates to remember an event,
these keepsakes are reminders of the loving hours spent.

ABCDEFGHIJKLM

NOPQRSTUVWXYZ

ANTIQUE ALPHABET

Alone in the attic
on an autumn afternoon,
I found this antique alphabet
alongside Grandma's loom.
It was tucked inside an album,
abandoned years ago;
which ancestor stitched this sampler,
I assume I'll never know.

Stitch Count: 123 × 163

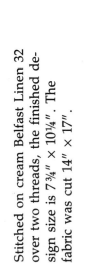

DESIGN SIZES

Aida 11   11⅛" × 14⅞"
Aida 14   8¾" × 11⅝"
Aida 18   6⅞" × 9"
Hardanger 22   5⅝" × 7⅞"

FABRICS

Aida 11
Aida 14
Aida 18
Hardanger 22

ANCHOR   DMC (used for sample)

Step One: Cross-stitch (two strands)

ANCHOR	DMC		
9		760	Salmon
11		3328	Salmon-med.
969	◄	316	Antique Mauve-med.
920	✕	932	Antique Blue-lt.
921	∴	931	Antique Blue-med.
876	○	502	Blue Green
878	E	501	Blue Green-dk.
379	■	840	Beige Brown-med.

Stitched on cream Belfast Linen 32 over two threads, the finished design size is 7¾" × 10¼". The fabric was cut 14" × 17".

ABCDEFGHIJKLM

BABY SAMPLER

You can begin this beautiful sampler
long before baby is born,
but leave enough blank space
for his or her name to adorn.
Whether it's Bobby or Betsy Sue,
just fill in the space for his name,
and this bright baby design
will be ready for a pink or blue frame.

CURTIS MURPHY
SEPT 23, 1900

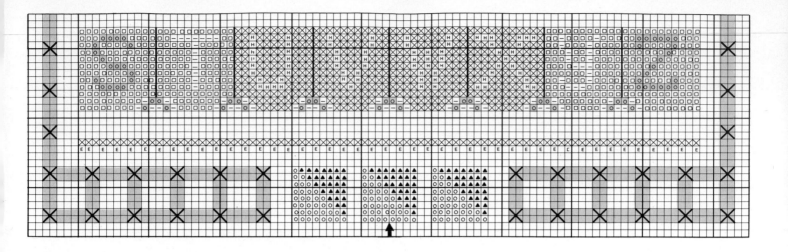

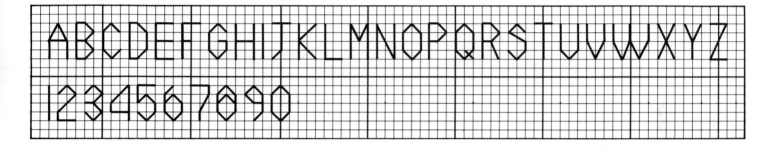

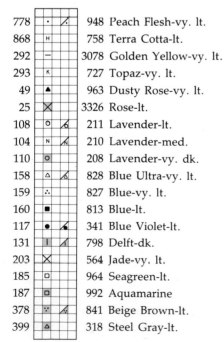

Stitched on white Aida 11 over one thread, the finished design size is 8⅞″ × 14⅜″. The fabric was cut 15″ × 21″. (See Suppliers for beads.)

ANCHOR **DMC** (used for sample)

Step One: Cross-stitch (three strands)

778		948 Peach Flesh-vy. lt.
868	H	758 Terra Cotta-lt.
292	–	3078 Golden Yellow-vy. lt.
293	K	727 Topaz-vy. lt.
49	▲	963 Dusty Rose-vy. lt.
25	✕	3326 Rose-lt.
108	○	211 Lavender-lt.
104	N	210 Lavender-med.
110	○	208 Lavender-vy. dk.
158	△	828 Blue Ultra-vy. lt.
159	∴	827 Blue-vy. lt.
160	■	813 Blue-lt.
117	●	341 Blue Violet-lt.
131	I	798 Delft-dk.
203	✕	564 Jade-vy. lt.
185	□	964 Seagreen-lt.
187	□	992 Aquamarine
378	∴	841 Beige Brown-lt.
399	△	318 Steel Gray-lt.

Step Two: Backstitch

| 131 | 798 Delft-dk., three strands (letters F through L) |
| 149 | 311 Navy Blue-med., one strand (all else) |

Step Three: French Knots (one strand)

| 149 | ● | 311 Navy Blue-med. |

Step Four: Beadwork

S	Pale Peach (MPR 148T)
+	Pink (MPR 145T)
E	Iris (MPR 252T)
P	Light Green (MPR 525K)
U	Christmas Green (MPR 167T)

Step Five: Satin Ribbonwork

A	Light Green ⅛″–wide (couched with matching floss, one strand)
B	Light Green ¹/₁₆″–wide (couched with matching floss, one strand)
C	Yellow ¹/₁₆″–wide
D	Peach ¹/₁₆″–wide
E	Light Green ¹/₁₆″–wide
F	Pink ¹/₁₆″–wide
G	Blue ¹/₁₆″–wide

| H | Lavender ¹/₁₆″–wide |
| I | Light Green ⅛″–wide (couched with matching ¹/₁₆″–wide ribbon) |

1. Lay ribbon in place on fabric. Thread each end to the wrong side. Tack ribbon ends together on wrong side of stitched piece, being careful not to pull ribbon too tightly; see Diagram 1.

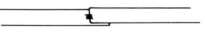

Diagram 1

2. Secure the ribbon by couching with thread; see Diagram 2. Individual couching lines are shown on the graph.

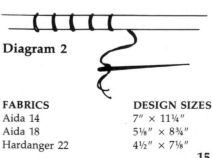

Diagram 2

FABRICS	DESIGN SIZES
Aida 14	7″ × 11¼″
Aida 18	5⅛″ × 8¾″
Hardanger 22	4½″ × 7⅛″

ABCDEFGHIJKLM

CONGRATULATIONS!

Say congratulations
with this cross-stitched creation,
perfect for commencement
or any celebration.
It's sure to be cherished
for all the care you've shown,
in complimenting their being
in a class all their own.

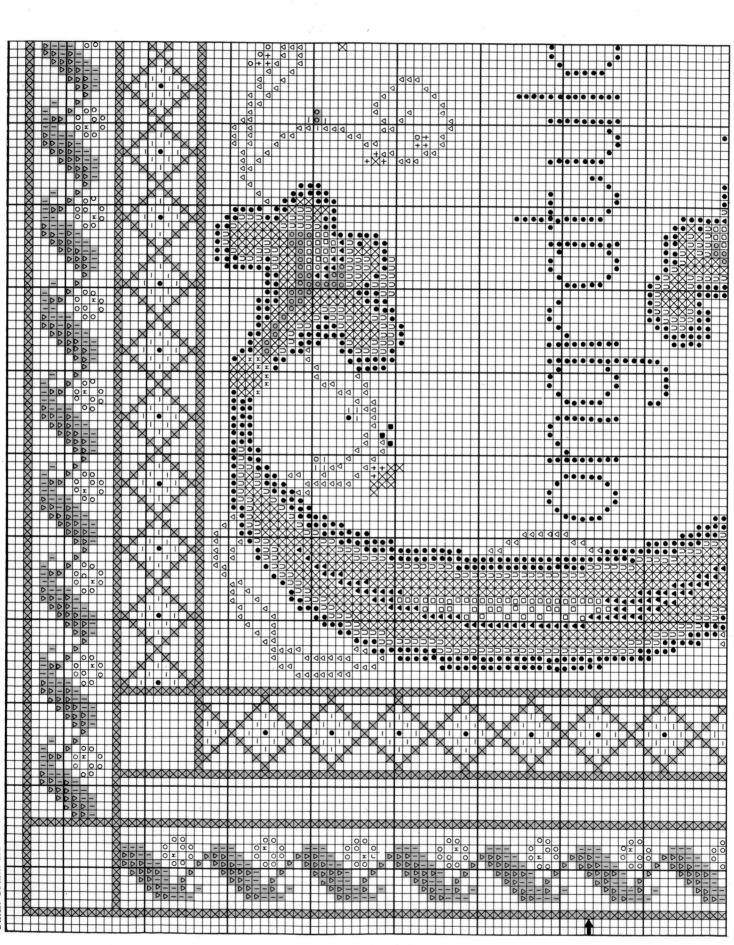

Stitch Count: 195 × 137

DESIGN SIZES

FABRICS	
Aida 11	17¾" × 12½"
Aida 14	13⅞" × 9¾"
Aida 18	10⅞" × 7⅝"
Hardanger 22	8⅞" × 6¼"

871	3041	Antique Violet-med.
928	598	Turquoise-lt.
167	597	Turquoise
168	518	Wedgewood-lt.
921	931	Antique Blue-med.
214	966	Baby Green-med.
213	504	Blue Green-lt.
875	503	Blue Green-med.
876	502	Blue Green
859	3053	Gray Green
846	3051	Gray Green-dk.
933	543	Beige Brown-ultra vy. lt.

Stitched on cream Belfast Linen 32 over two threads, the finished design size is 12¼" × 8½". The fabric was cut 19" × 15".

ANCHOR   DMC (used for sample)

Step One: Cross-stitch (two strands)

868	758	Terra-Cotta-lt.
893	224	Shell Pink-lt.
894	223	Shell Pink-med.
969	316	Antique Mauve-med.
970	315	Antique Mauve-dk.
869	3042	Antique Violet-lt.

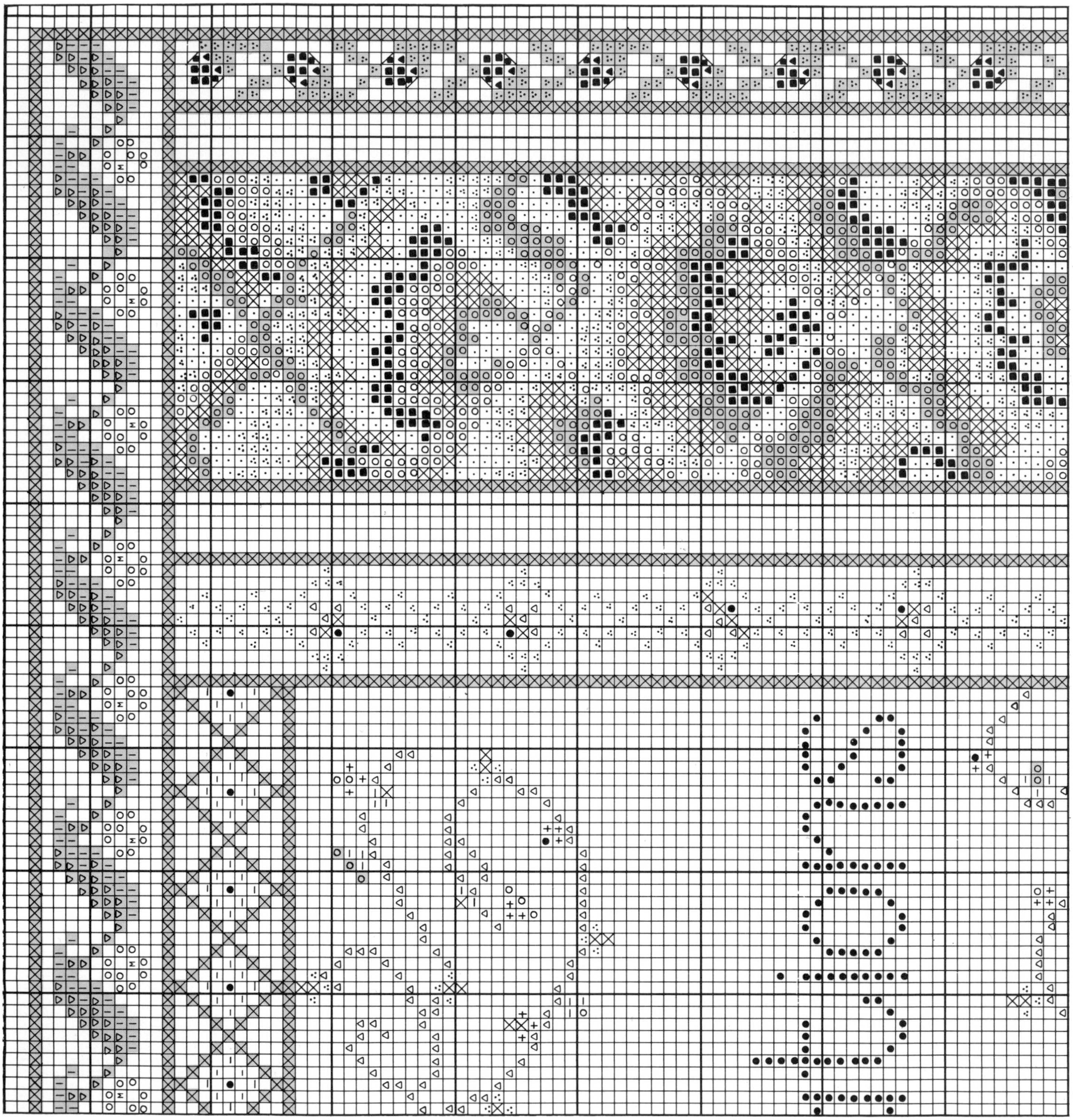

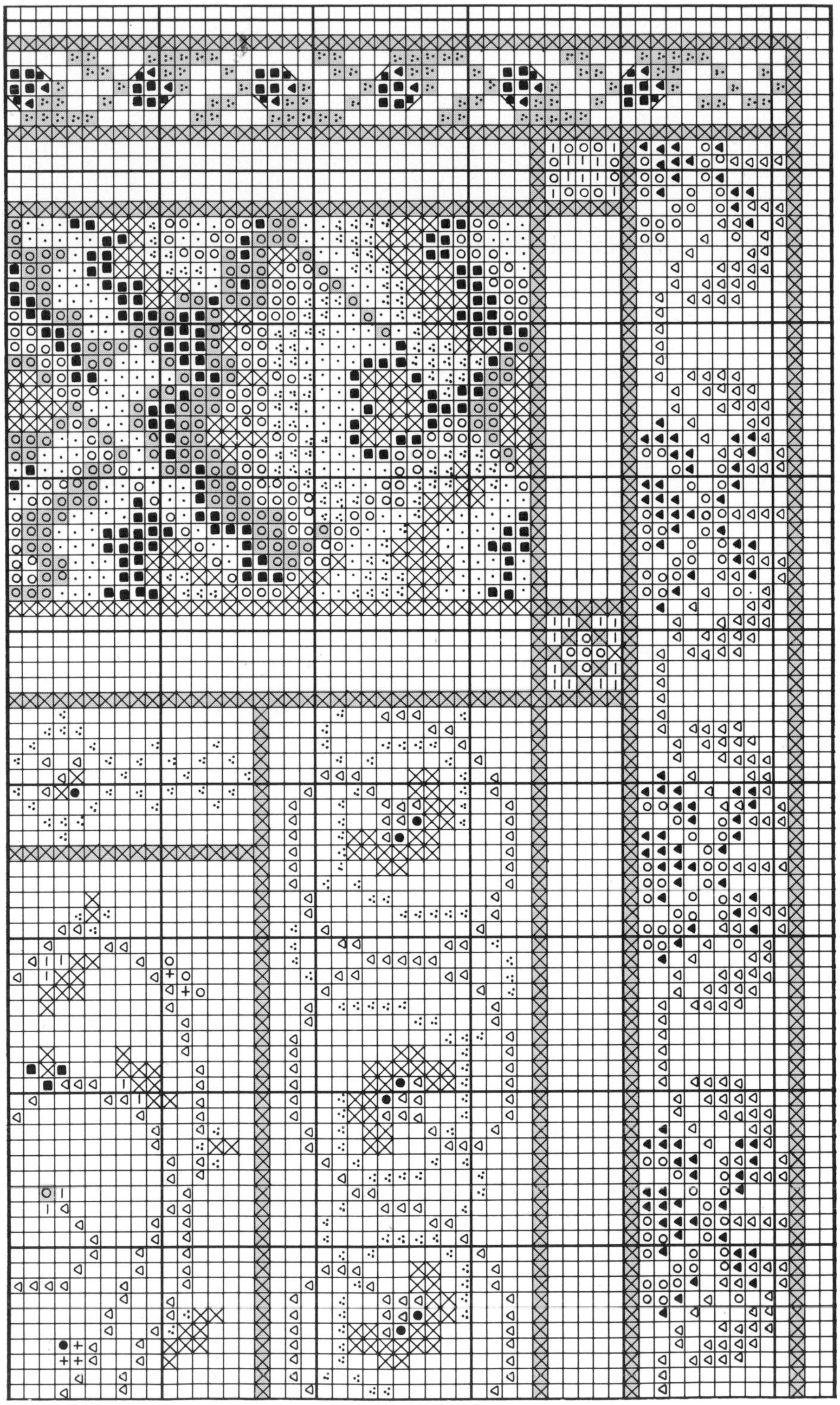

abcDEFGHIJKLM

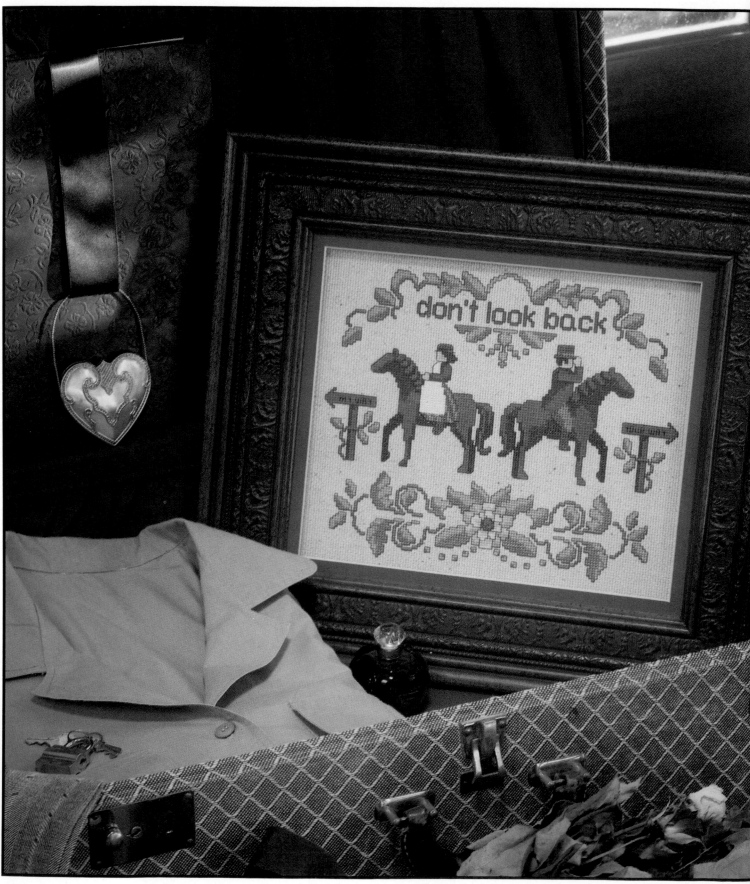

DON'T LOOK BACK

Draw up your horse and declare a new day;

with directions and determination, you'll sure find your way.

Though the distance may seem long and dreary days turn blue,

don't drift, make decisions, and your dreams will all come true!

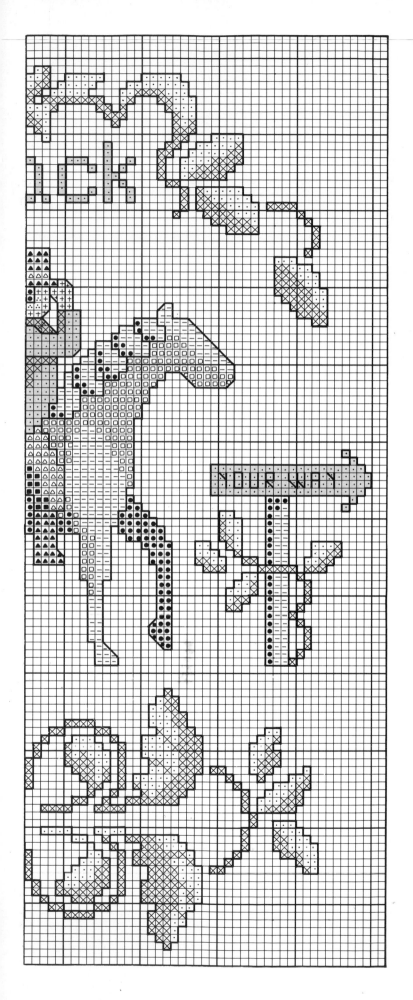

Stitched on Rustico 14 over one thread, the finished design size is 9¾" × 8⅜". The fabric was cut 16" × 15".

ANCHOR			DMC (used for sample)

Step One: Cross-stitch (two strands)

1	o	⟋	White
301	I		744 Yellow-pale
891	▽		676 Old Gold-lt.
890	∷		729 Old Gold-med.
4146	+	⟋	754 Peach Flesh-lt.
8	∴		761 Salmon-lt.
11	·	⟋	3328 Salmon-med.
13	X	⟋	347 Salmon-dk.
921	△		931 Antique Blue-med.
922	■		930 Antique Blue-dk.
843	·		3364 Pine Green
861	X		3363 Pine Green-med.
349	–	⟋	301 Mahogany-med.
351	□	⟋	400 Mahogany-dk.
352	●	⟋	300 Mahogany-vy. dk.
401	▲	⟋	413 Pewter Gray-dk.

Step Two: Backstitch (one strand)

922		930 Antique Blue-dk. (skirt, pants, top of apron)
862		3362 Pine Green-dk. (leaves, stems)
381		938 Coffee Brown-ultra dk. (lettering on signs)
401		413 Pewter Gray-dk. (hats, boots)
352		300 Mahogany-vy. dk. (all else)

FABRICS	DESIGN SIZES
Aida 11	12⅜" × 10⅝"
Aida 14	9¾" × 8⅜"
Aida 18	7½" × 6½"
Hardanger 22	6⅛" × 5⅜"

ABCDEFGHIJKLM

EGGS BY THE DOZEN

My mother bought a dozen eggs,
then went out to exercise;
evidently upon returning home,
she got a big surprise.
The carton she found was empty;
then something caught her eye;
what emerged was a dozen chicks,
each no bigger than 1″ high.

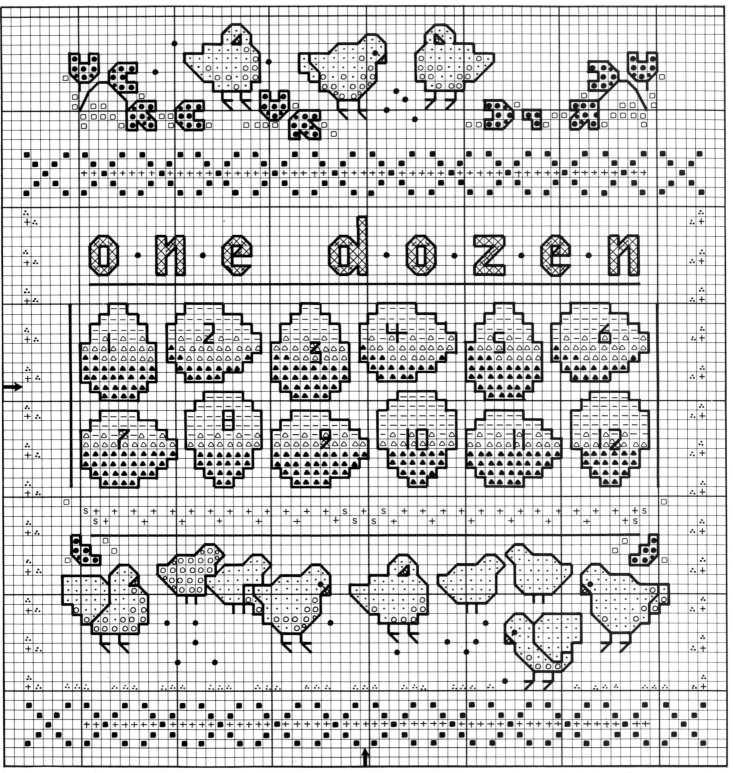

Stitched on terra-cotta Lugana 25 over two threads, the finished design size is 5⅝" × 6". The fabric was cut 12" × 12".

ANCHOR   **DMC** (used for sample)

Step One: Cross-stitch (two strands)

1	−		White
926	△		Ecru
881	▪		945 Sportsman Flesh
5968	● /		355 Terra-Cotta-dk.
885	▲		739 Tan-ultra vy. lt.
886	· /		677 Old Gold-vy. lt.
891	○ /		676 Old Gold-lt.
920	+		932 Antique Blue-lt.
922	s		930 Antique Blue-dk.
216	□		367 Pistachio Green-dk.
379	∴		840 Beige Brown-med.
380	✕ /		838 Beige Brown-vy. dk.

Step Two: Backstitch (one strand)

8	353 Peach Flesh (flowers)
885	739 Tan-ultra vy. lt. (eggs, border)
216	367 Pistachio Green-dk. (stems)
380	838 Beige Brown-vy. dk. (all else)

Step Three: French Knots (one strand)

380	838 Beige Brown-vy. dk.

FABRICS   **DESIGN SIZES**
Aida 11   6½" × 6⅞"
Aida 14   5⅛" × 5⅜"
Aida 18   4" × 4⅛"
Hardanger 22   3¼" × 3⅜"

FARM FULL OF ANIMALS

The farmer forgot to put out feed and his barnyard friends were famished;
upon arriving at the field the next day, he found that they had vanished.
He finally found them pouting—and begged them to come home;
now they feast on five-course meals and occasionally dine in Rome!

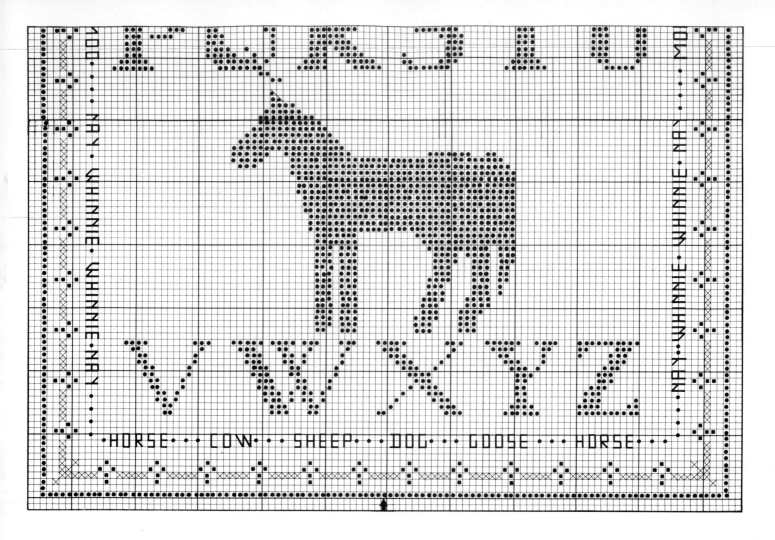

Stitched on Glenshee Linen Natural 29 over two threads, the finished design size is 7½″ × 15½″. The fabric was cut 14″ × 22″.

ANCHOR **DMC** (used for sample)

Step One: Cross-stitch (two strands)

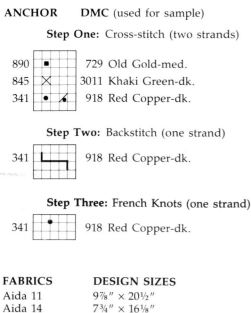

890	729 Old Gold-med.
845	3011 Khaki Green-dk.
341	918 Red Copper-dk.

Step Two: Backstitch (one strand)

341 | 918 Red Copper-dk.

Step Three: French Knots (one strand)

341 | 918 Red Copper-dk.

FABRICS **DESIGN SIZES**
Aida 11   9⅞″ × 20½″
Aida 14   7¾″ × 16⅛″
Aida 18   6″ × 12½″
Hardanger 22   5″ × 10¼″

ABCDEFGHIJKLM

GARDEN DREAMS

Mary, Mary, quite contemporary, how does your garden grow?
"There are geraniums and morning glories and daffodils in a row.
When asked why I grow only flowers, and vegetables no more,
I reply, 'My goodness, I can get frozen greens at any convenience store!' "

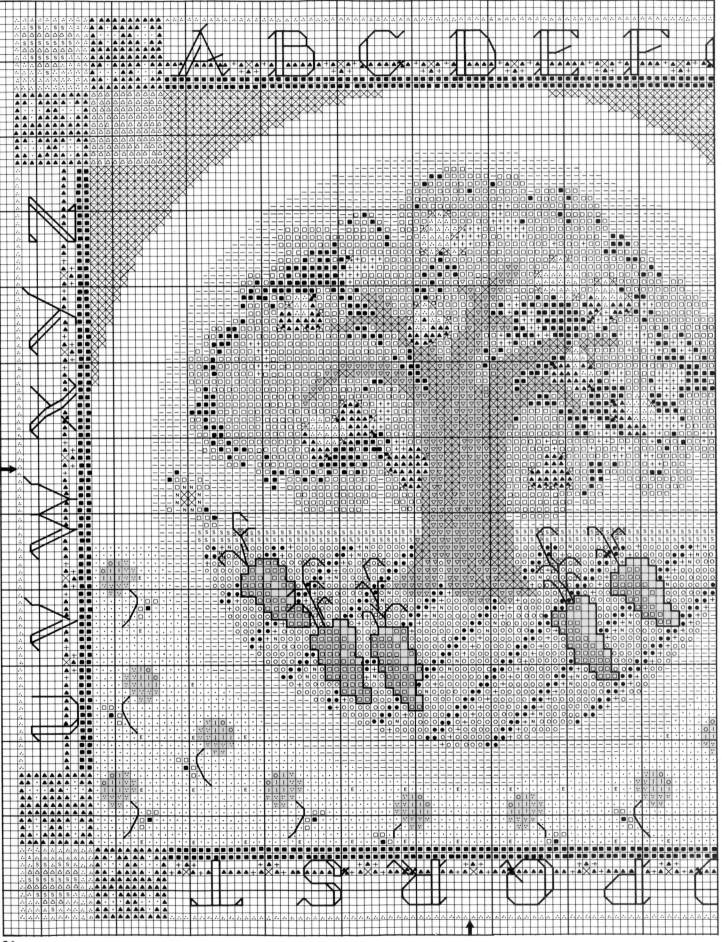

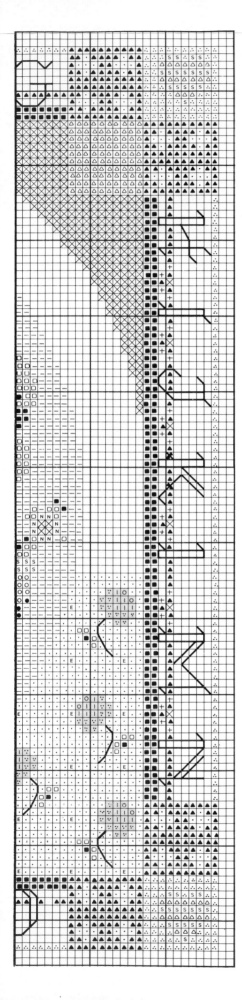

Stitched on white Belfast Linen 32 over two threads, the finished design size is 7½" × 7½". The fabric was cut 14" × 14". (See Suppliers for beads.)

ANCHOR   **DMC** (used for sample)

Step One: Cross-stitch (two strands)

ANCHOR			DMC	
295	∴	⁄	726	Topaz-lt.
306	▲	⁄	725	Topaz
323	▨		722	Orange Spice-lt.
324	▢		721	Orange Spice-med.
49	✕		963	Dusty Rose-vy. lt.
59	N		326	Rose-vy. deep
108	I		211	Lavender-lt.
105	○		209	Lavender-dk.
110	∵		208	Lavender-vy. dk.
158	△		747	Sky Blue-vy. lt.
158	–		747	Sky Blue-vy. lt. (one strand)
185	s		964	Seagreen-lt.
120	·		794	Cornflower Blue-lt.
265	○		3348	Yellow Green-lt.
267	●		470	Avocado Green-lt.
256	+	⁄	704	Chartreuse-bright
210	■	⁄	562	Jade-med.
923	▫	⁄	699	Christmas Green
903	▽	⁄	3032	Mocha Brown-med.
380	✕	⁄	839	Beige Brown-dk.

Step Two: Backstitch (one strand)

121		793 Cornflower Blue-med. (alphabet)
923		699 Christmas Green (all else)

Step Three: Beadwork

E	Pink (MPR 145T)

FABRICS	DESIGN SIZES
Aida 11	10⅞" × 10⅞"
Aida 14	8⅝" × 8⅝"
Aida 18	6⅝" × 6⅝"
Hardanger 22	5½" × 5½"

ABCDEFG**H**IJKLM

HOME

I remember all the holidays
and Mother's homemade pie;
the hideaway I helped Dad build
reached halfway to the sky.
Throughout my head, the highlights
of my life will happily roam,
until I reach ol' Humbleville,
the place that I call home.

Stitch Count: **150 × 97**

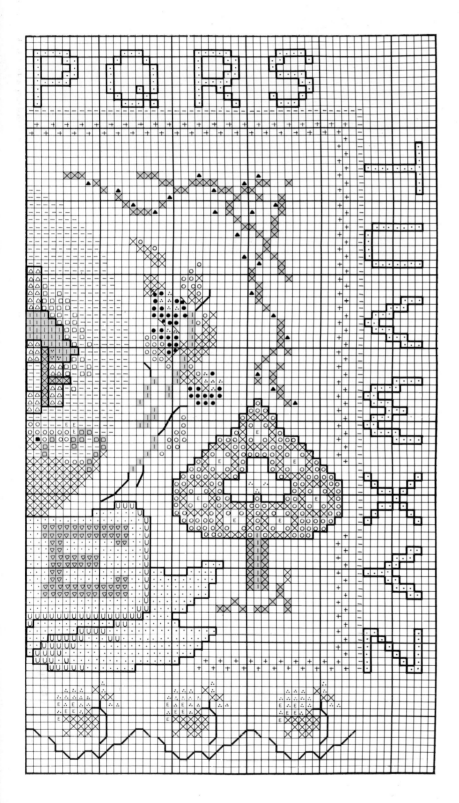

Stitched on cream Belfast Linen 32 over two threads, the finished design size is 9⅜" × 6". The fabric was cut 16" × 12". (See Suppliers for beads.)

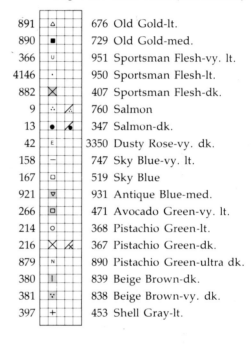

ANCHOR		DMC (used for sample)	
		Step One: Cross-stitch (two strands)	
891	△	676	Old Gold-lt.
890	■	729	Old Gold-med.
366	U	951	Sportsman Flesh-vy. lt.
4146	·	950	Sportsman Flesh-lt.
882	⊠	407	Sportsman Flesh-dk.
9	∴ ╱	760	Salmon
13	● ◢	347	Salmon-dk.
42	E	3350	Dusty Rose-vy. dk.
158	−	747	Sky Blue-vy. lt.
167	▫	519	Sky Blue
921	▽	931	Antique Blue-med.
266	▱	471	Avocado Green-vy. lt.
214	○	368	Pistachio Green-lt.
216	✕ ╱	367	Pistachio Green-dk.
879	N	890	Pistachio Green-ultra dk.
380	‖	839	Beige Brown-dk.
381	⋰	838	Beige Brown-vy. dk.
397	+	453	Shell Gray-lt.

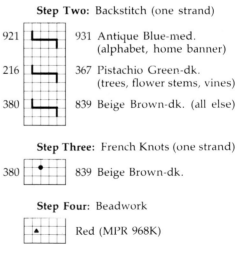

Step Two: Backstitch (one strand)

921		931	Antique Blue-med. (alphabet, home banner)
216		367	Pistachio Green-dk. (trees, flower stems, vines)
380		839	Beige Brown-dk. (all else)

Step Three: French Knots (one strand)

380	●	839	Beige Brown-dk.

Step Four: Beadwork

▲	Red (MPR 968K)

FABRICS	DESIGN SIZES
Aida 11	13¾" × 8⅞"
Aida 14	10¾" × 6⅞"
Aida 18	8⅜" × 5⅜"
Hardanger 22	6⅞" × 4⅜"

ABCDEFGHIJKLM

I WANT EWE

I included a bit of irony
to add some sensation,
in hopes this idea
might arouse your imagination.
My illustration initially was
just red, white, and blue.
but indescribably turned out to say,
"I want ewe!"

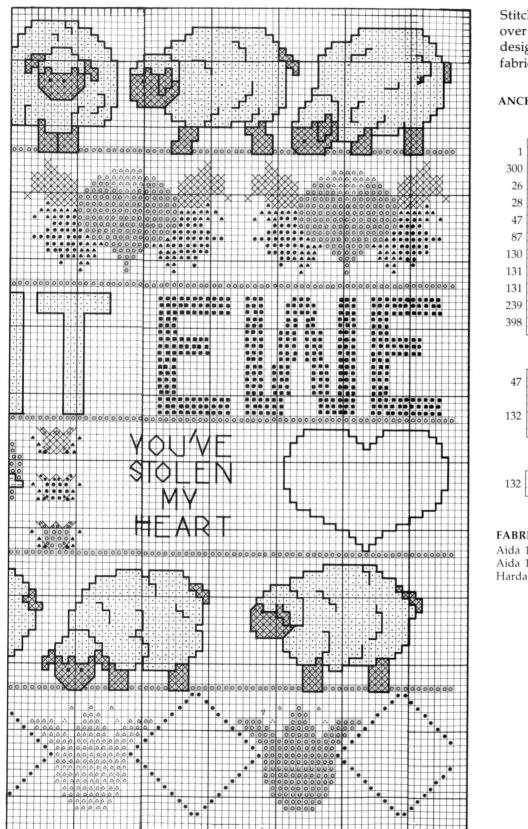

Stitched on light blue Aida 14 over one thread, the finished design size is 12⅛" × 8½". The fabric was cut 19" × 15".

ANCHOR   **DMC** (used for sample)

Step One: Cross-stitch (two strands)

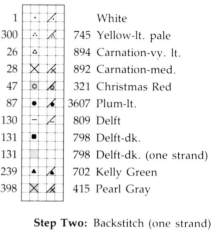

1		White
300		745 Yellow-lt. pale
26		894 Carnation-vy. lt.
28		892 Carnation-med.
47		321 Christmas Red
87		3607 Plum-lt.
130		809 Delft
131		798 Delft-dk.
131		798 Delft-dk. (one strand)
239		702 Kelly Green
398		415 Pearl Gray

Step Two: Backstitch (one strand)

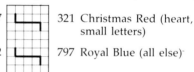

47		321 Christmas Red (heart, small letters)
132		797 Royal Blue (all else)

Step Three: French Knots (one strand)

132	●	797 Royal Blue

FABRICS	**DESIGN SIZES**
Aida 11	15½" × 10⅞"
Aida 18	9½" × 6⅝"
Hardanger 22	7¾" × 5⅜"

ABCDEFGHI J KLM

JACK-IN-THE-BOX

At the end of the jazzy jingle, Jack jumped out with glee;
the birds joined in to celebrate the summer jubilee.
This jester recited poetry as he juggled each balloon,
and joked about being jollier than St. Nicholas in June.

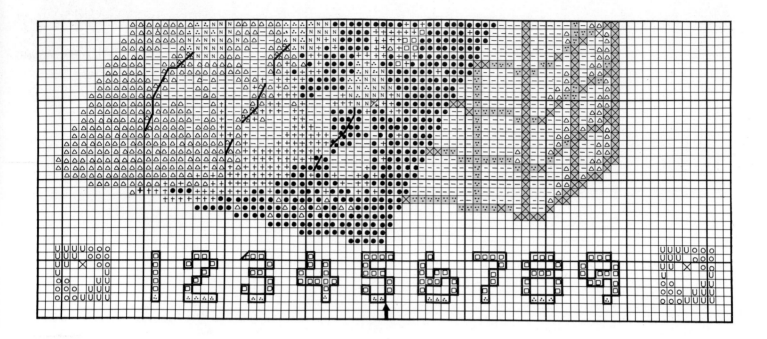

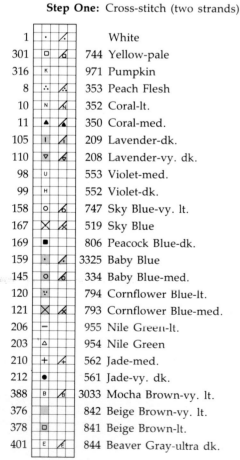

Stitched on white Aida 14 over one thread, the finished design size is 5⅞" × 10¼". The fabric was cut 12" × 17".

ANCHOR **DMC** (used for sample)

Step One: Cross-stitch (two strands)

1			White
301			744 Yellow-pale
316			971 Pumpkin
8			353 Peach Flesh
10			352 Coral-lt.
11			350 Coral-med.
105			209 Lavender-dk.
110			208 Lavender-vy. dk.
98			553 Violet-med.
99			552 Violet-dk.
158			747 Sky Blue-vy. lt.
167			519 Sky Blue
169			806 Peacock Blue-dk.
159			3325 Baby Blue
145			334 Baby Blue-med.
120			794 Cornflower Blue-lt.
121			793 Cornflower Blue-med.
206			955 Nile Green-lt.
203			954 Nile Green
210			562 Jade-med.
212			561 Jade-vy. dk.
388			3033 Mocha Brown-vy. lt.
376			842 Beige Brown-vy. lt.
378			841 Beige Brown-lt.
401			844 Beaver Gray-ultra dk.

Step Two: Backstitch (one strand)

10		352 Coral-lt. (numbers)
169		806 Peacock Blue-dk. (alphabet, stripes on balloon)
940		792 Cornflower Blue-dk. (balloon strings, flower stems)
401		844 Beaver Gray-ultra dk. (face)

Step Three: French Knots (one strand)

169		806 Peacock Blue-dk.

FABRICS	**DESIGN SIZES**
Aida 11	7½" × 13"
Aida 18	4½" × 8"
Hardanger 22	3¾" × 6½"

ABCDEFGHIJKLM

KITCHEN KUILTS

Quilts, as you know,
are usually spelled with a "Q,"
but these kuilts are kept
in the kitchen to view.
So, if the coffee's knocked over
and the kettle starts steaming,
these kuilts with a "K"
keep your kitchen agleaming.

Stitch Count: **43 × 51**

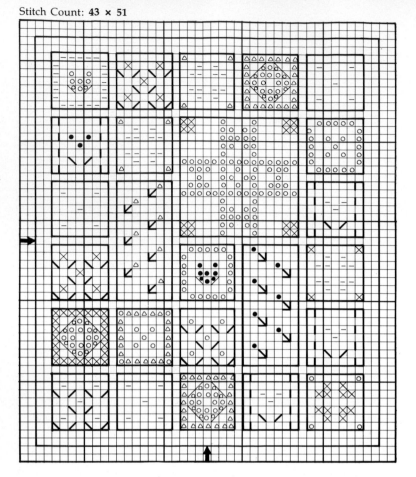

Stitched on cream Jobelan 28 over two threads, the finished size for each design is 3⅛" × 3⅝". The fabric was cut 10" × 10" for each.

ANCHOR   **DMC** (used for sample)

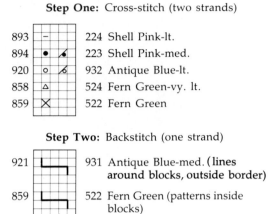

Step One: Cross-stitch (two strands)

893	–		224 Shell Pink-lt.
894	•	✎	223 Shell Pink-med.
920	o	✎	932 Antique Blue-lt.
858	△		524 Fern Green-vy. lt.
859	✕		522 Fern Green

Step Two: Backstitch (one strand)

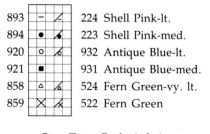

921 — 931 Antique Blue-med. (lines around blocks, outside border)

859 — 522 Fern Green (patterns inside blocks)

Stitch Count: **43 × 51**

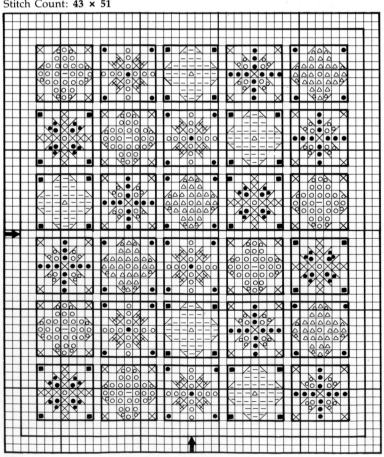

ANCHOR   **DMC** (used for sample)

Step One: Cross-stitch (two strands)

893	–	✎	224 Shell Pink-lt.
894	•	✎	223 Shell Pink-med.
920	o	✎	932 Antique Blue-lt.
921	■		931 Antique Blue-med.
858	△	✎	524 Fern Green-vy. lt.
859	✕	✎	522 Fern Green

Step Two: Backstitch (one strand)

921 — 931 Antique Blue-med.

Stitch Count: **43 × 51**

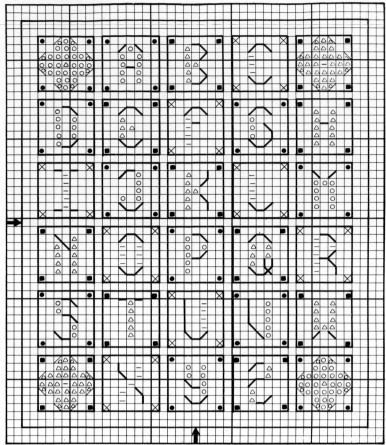

ANCHOR   DMC (used for sample)

Step One: Cross-stitch (two strands)

893	−	224 Shell Pink-lt.
894	●	223 Shell Pink-med.
920	o ⟋	932 Antique Blue-lt.
921	■	931 Antique Blue-med.
858	△ ⟋	524 Fern Green-vy. lt.
859	✕	522 Fern Green

Step Two: Backstitch (one strand)

893		224 Shell Pink-lt. (pink letters)
920		932 Antique Blue-lt. (blue letters)
921		931 Antique Blue-med. (lines around blocks, outside border)
858		524 Fern Green-vy. lt. (green letters)

FABRICS   **DESIGN SIZES**
Aida 11   4″ × 4⅝″
Aida 14   3⅛″ × 3⅝″
Aida 18   2⅜″ × 2⅞″
Hardanger 22   2″ × 2⅜″

ABCDEFGHIJKLM

LOVE SONG

There was a lord from London
who was very much alone;
then he received a letter
from a lady in Cologne.
She was looking for a lover
and insisted he be loyal;
she cared less about his looks
but hoped his family line was royal!

Stitch Count: **113 × 130**

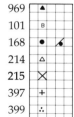
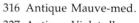
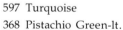

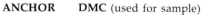

Stitched on black Hardanger 22 over two threads, the finished design size is 10¼″ × 11⅞″. The fabric was cut 17″ × 18″.

ANCHOR		DMC (used for sample)

Step One: Cross-stitch (three strands)

892	·	819 Baby Pink-lt.
49	−	963 Dusty Rose-vy. lt.
25	o	3326 Rose-lt.
27	■	899 Rose-med.
42	E	309 Rose-deep
968	□	778 Antique Mauve-lt.

969	▲	316 Antique Mauve-med.
101	B	327 Antique Violet-dk.
168	● /	597 Turquoise
214	△	368 Pistachio Green-lt.
215	X	320 Pistachio Green-med.
397	+	453 Shell Gray-lt.
399	∴	451 Shell Gray-dk.

Step Two: Backstitch (one strand)

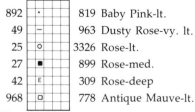

27		899 Rose-med. (pattern in left panel)
42		309 Rose-deep (border lines, flower petals)

215		320 Pistachio Green-med. (small flower stems)
399		451 Shell Gray-dk. (all else)

FABRICS — **DESIGN SIZES**

Aida 11	10¼″ × 11⅞″
Aida 14	8½″ × 9¼″
Aida 18	6¼″ × 7¼″
Hardanger 22	5⅛″ × 5⅞″

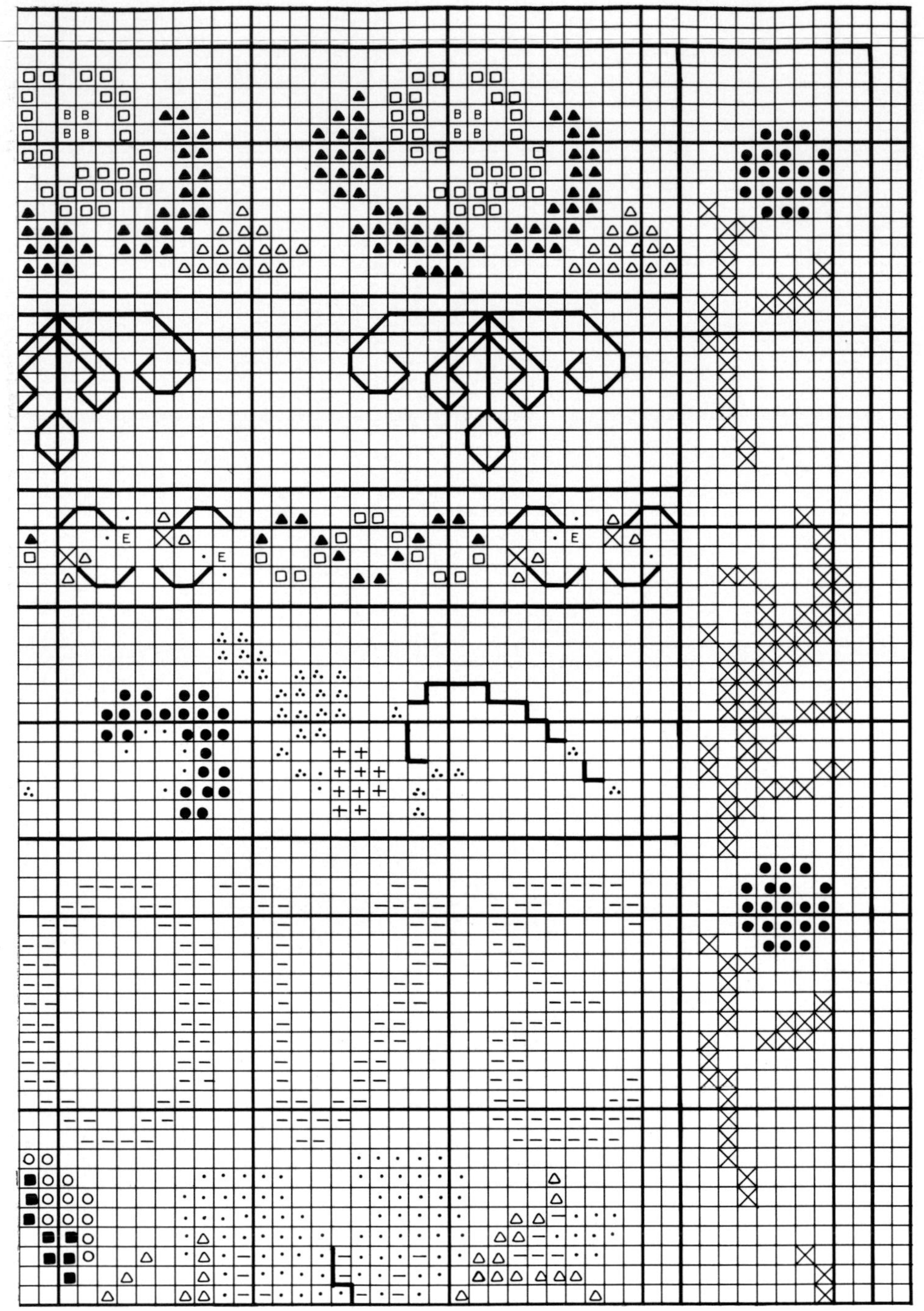

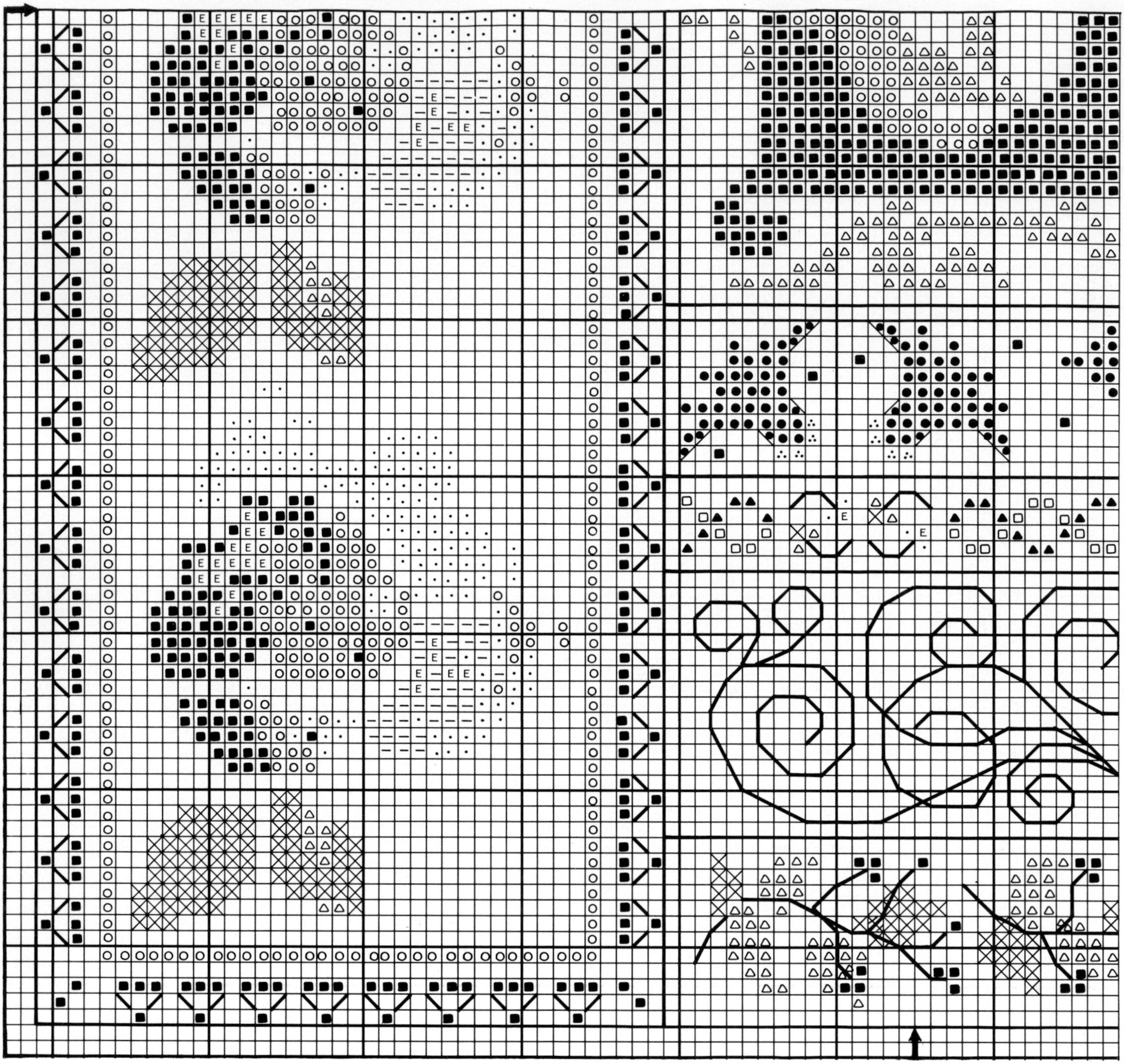

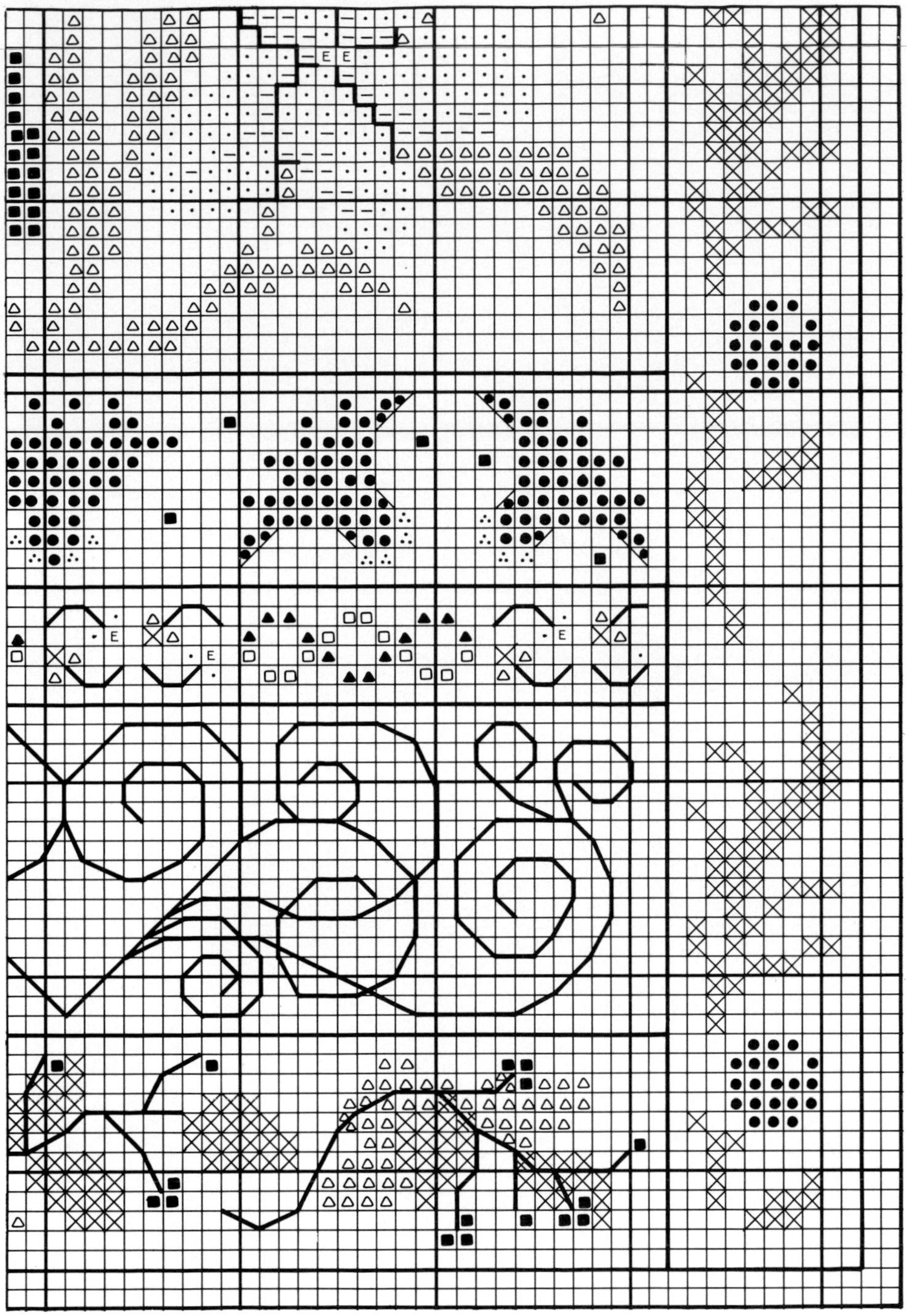

ABCDEFGHIJKL M

M IS FOR MOTHER

M could be for Margaret,
my friend in second grade.
M might be for Miss Martha,
our most meticulous maid.
M may be for Mrs. Mitchell,
the neighbor we all fear.
But this M's for my mom,
the mother-of-the-year!

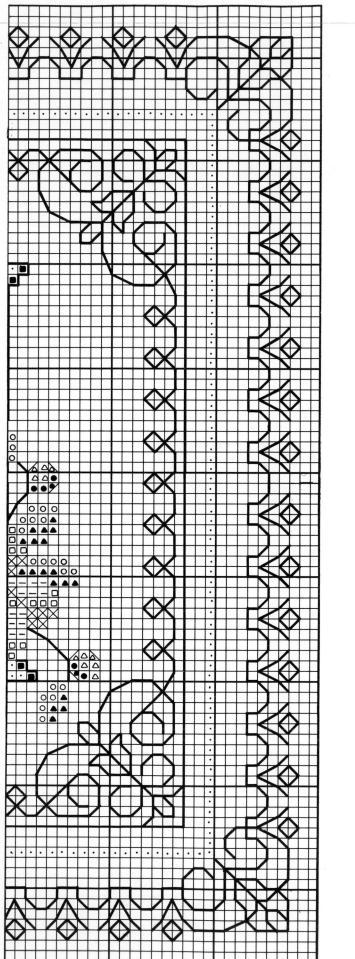

Stitched on white Belfast Linen 32 over two threads, the finished design size is 5⅞" × 5½". The fabric was cut 12" × 12".

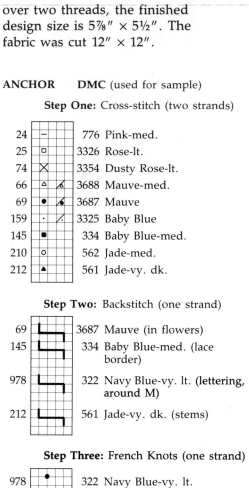

ANCHOR   DMC (used for sample)

Step One: Cross-stitch (two strands)

24	–	776 Pink-med.
25	□	3326 Rose-lt.
74	X	3354 Dusty Rose-lt.
66	△ ◸	3688 Mauve-med.
69	● ◿	3687 Mauve
159	· ◹	3325 Baby Blue
145	▪	334 Baby Blue-med.
210	○	562 Jade-med.
212	▲	561 Jade-vy. dk.

Step Two: Backstitch (one strand)

69	3687 Mauve (in flowers)
145	334 Baby Blue-med. (lace border)
978	322 Navy Blue-vy. lt. (lettering, around M)
212	561 Jade-vy. dk. (stems)

Step Three: French Knots (one strand)

978	322 Navy Blue-vy. lt.

FABRICS   **DESIGN SIZES**
Aida 11   8½" × 8"
Aida 14   6¾" × 6¼"
Aida 18   5¼" × 4⅞"
Hardanger 22   4¼" × 4"

NOPQRSTUVWXYZ

NOW I KNOW MY ABCs

First my nanny taught me numbers — one, two, and three —
and then a nutty nursery rhyme with letters A to Z
about an alligator bowling and an onion for a pet.
Even though it's mostly nonsense, now I know my alphabet!

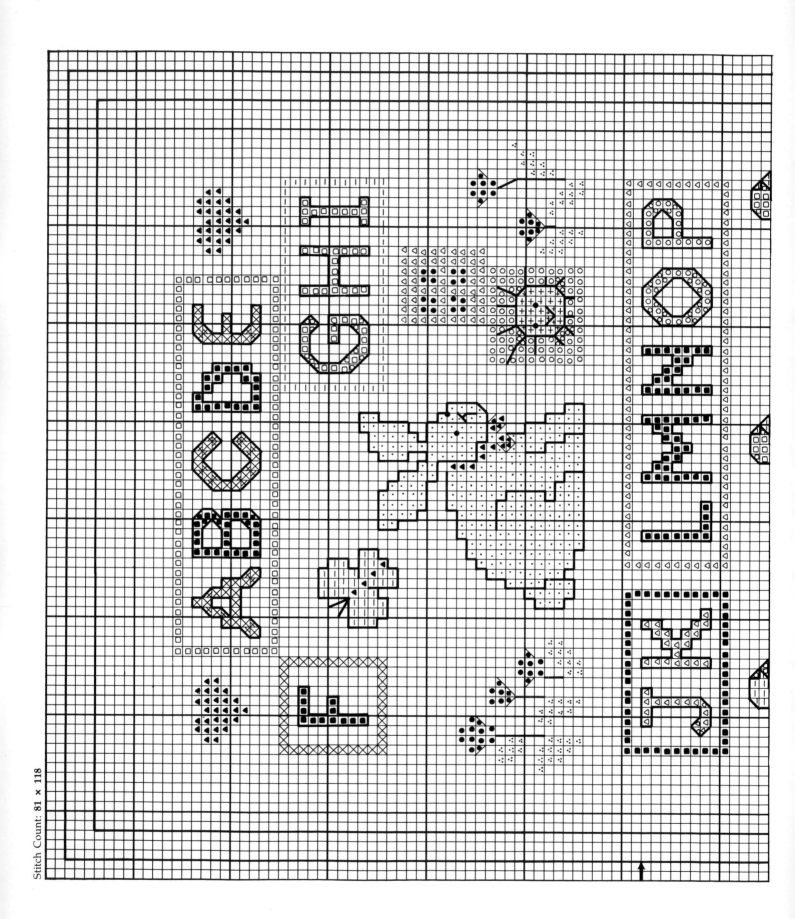

Stitch Count: **81 × 118**

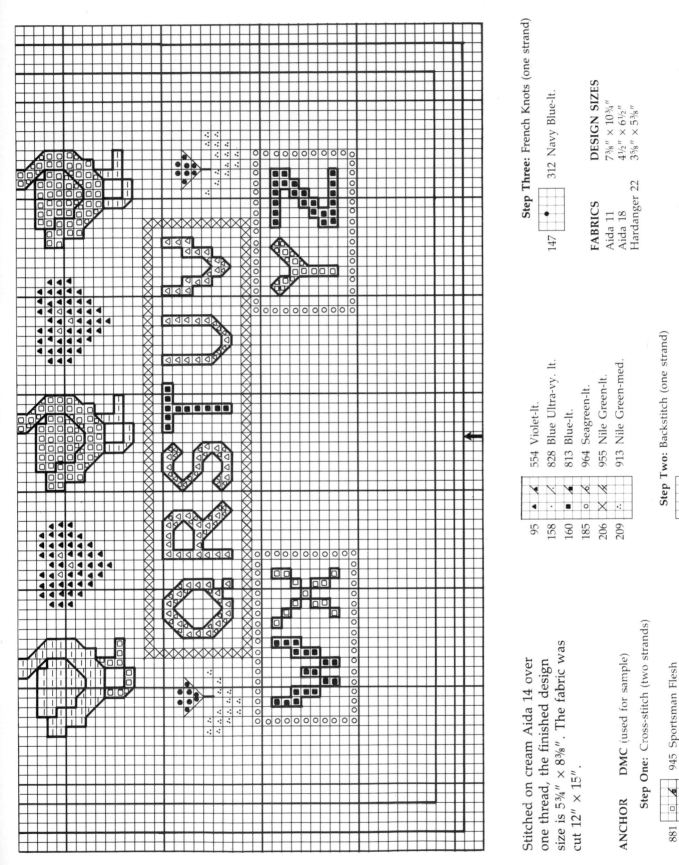

Stitched on cream Aida 14 over one thread, the finished design size is 5¾" × 8⅜". The fabric was cut 12" × 15".

ANCHOR   DMC (used for sample)

Step One: Cross-stitch (two strands)

881	□	◢	945 Sportsman Flesh
292	+	◢	3078 Golden Yellow-vy. lt.
74	−	◢	3354 Dusty Rose-lt.
42	●	◢	3350 Dusty Rose-vy. dk.
108	△	◢	211 Lavender-lt.

95		◣	554 Violet-lt.
158	·	╱	828 Blue Ultra-vy. lt.
160	■	◪	813 Blue-lt.
185	○	◞	964 Seagreen-lt.
206	✕	◸	955 Nile Green-lt.
209	∴		913 Nile Green-med.

Step Two: Backstitch (one strand)

209	⌐	913 Nile Green-med. (stems)
160	⌐	813 Blue-lt. (border)
147	⌐	312 Navy Blue-lt. (all else)

Step Three: French Knots (one strand)

147	●	312 Navy Blue-lt.

DESIGN SIZES

FABRICS
Aida 11   7⅞" × 10¾"
Aida 18   4½" × 6½"
Hardanger 22 3⅝" × 5⅜"

There's a magic in the distance,
where the sea-line meets the sky.

OCEAN BLUE

There's a magic in the distance
where the sea-line meets the sky,
with oyster shells and octopuses,
the ospreys flying high.
The origin of the ocean blue
will always be a mystery,
but the day the ocean opened wide
is written down in history.

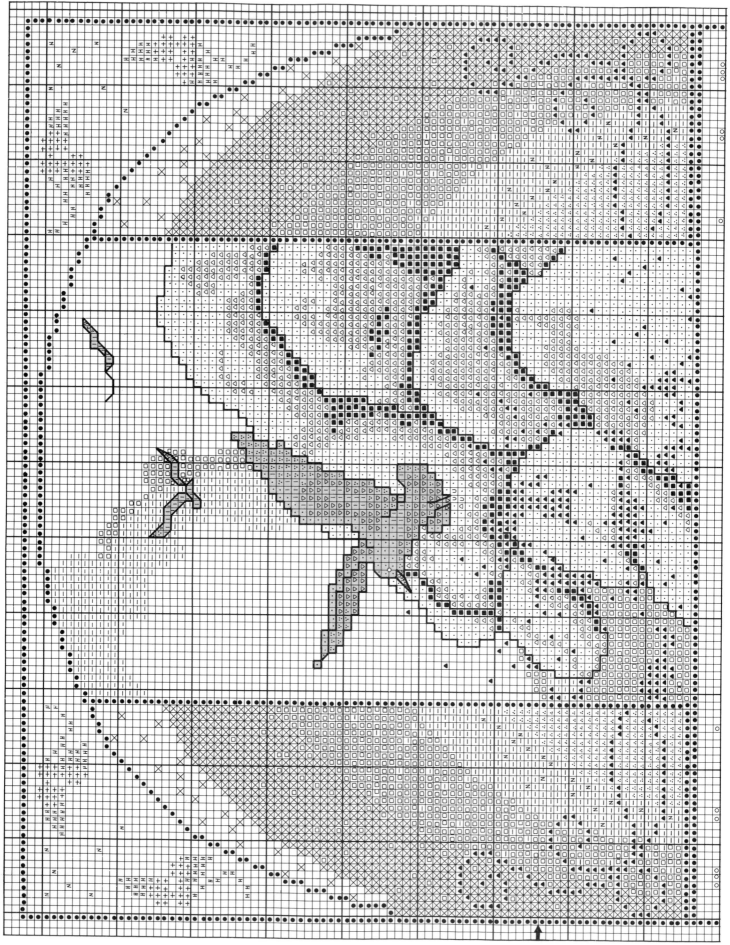

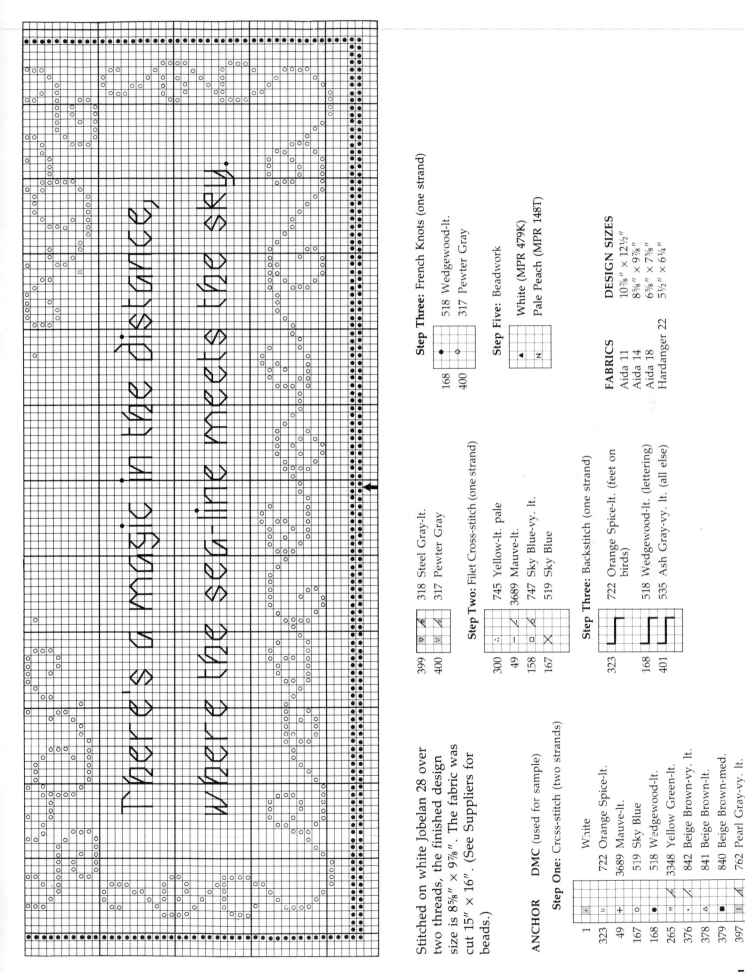

Stitched on white Jobelan 28 over two threads, the finished design size is 8⅝" × 9⅞". The fabric was cut 15" × 16". (See Suppliers for beads.)

ANCHOR   DMC (used for sample)

Step One: Cross-stitch (two strands)

1		White
323	∪	722 Orange Spice-lt.
49	+	3689 Mauve-lt.
167	○	519 Sky Blue
168	●	518 Wedgewood-lt.
265	H	3348 Yellow Green-lt.
376	.	842 Beige Brown-vy. lt.
378	△	841 Beige Brown-lt.
379	■	840 Beige Brown-med.
397	∕	762 Pearl Gray-vy. lt.

399		318 Steel Gray-lt.
400		317 Pewter Gray

Step Two: Filet Cross-stitch (one strand)

300	∷	745 Yellow-lt. pale
49	—	3689 Mauve-lt.
158	□	747 Sky Blue-vy. lt.
167	X	519 Sky Blue

Step Three: Backstitch (one strand)

323		722 Orange Spice-lt. (feet on birds)
168		518 Wedgewood-lt. (lettering)
401		535 Ash Gray-vy. lt. (all else)

Step Three: French Knots (one strand)

168	●	518 Wedgewood-lt.
400	○	317 Pewter Gray

Step Five: Beadwork

	◄	White (MPR 479K)
	N	Pale Peach (MPR 148T)

FABRICS   DESIGN SIZES

Aida 11   10⅞" × 12½"
Aida 14   8⅝" × 9⅞"
Aida 18   6⅝" × 7⅞"
Hardanger 22   5½" × 6¼"

ABCDEFGHIJKLM

PEGASUS

This palette of pastel colors was planned especially for the charade,

in which this winged-horse prances proudly in his very own parade.

As he pirouettes before the crowd, he is pointed out by all;

in the middle of his march we heard, ''He'd be perfect for my wall!''

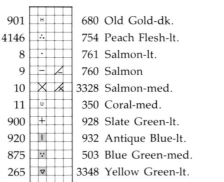

Stitched on cream Belfast Linen 32 over two threads, the finished design size is 7⅞″ × 10¼″. The fabric was cut 14″ × 17″. (See Suppliers for beads.)

ANCHOR   DMC (used for sample)

Step One: Cross-stitch (two strands)

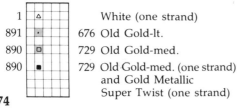

1		White (one strand)
891		676 Old Gold-lt.
890		729 Old Gold-med.
890		729 Old Gold-med. (one strand) and Gold Metallic Super Twist (one strand)

901		680 Old Gold-dk.
4146		754 Peach Flesh-lt.
8		761 Salmon-lt.
9		760 Salmon
10		3328 Salmon-med.
11		350 Coral-med.
900		928 Slate Green-lt.
920		932 Antique Blue-lt.
875		503 Blue Green-med.
265		3348 Yellow Green-lt.

843		3364 Pine Green
861		3363 Pine Green-med.
942		738 Tan-vy. lt.
362		437 Tan-lt.
309		435 Brown-vy. lt.
370		434 Brown-lt.
371		433 Brown-med.
888		371 Mustard
375		420 Hazel Nut Brown-dk.
900		3024 Brown Gray-vy. lt.

Step Two: Backstitch (one strand)

10	3328 Salmon-med. (alphabet)
11	350 Coral-med. (saddle)
309	435 Brown-vy. lt. (mane, tail)
371	433 Brown-med. (all else)

Step Three: Beadwork

Red (MPR 968K)

Step Four: Tassels

9   760 Salmon

Step Five: Couching (inside mane and tail; see photo)

9	760 Salmon (laid thread, three strands)
11	350 Coral-med. (couching thread)

To make a tassel, cut one 18″ piece and two 5″ pieces of salmon floss. Wrap the 18″ piece around two fingers. Thread a 5″ piece through loops; knot securely. Wrap the second 5″ piece tightly around the top of the loops near the knot; secure. Cut the fold in the loops opposite the knot. Trim to desired length. Repeat for remaining tassels. Tack to design where indicated.

For couching instructions, see Diagram 2 of " Baby Sampler", page 15; substitute thread for ribbon.

FABRICS	DESIGN SIZES
Aida 11	11½″ × 14⅞″
Aida 14	9″ × 11⅝″
Aida 18	7″ × 9″
Hardanger 22	5¾″ × 7⅜″

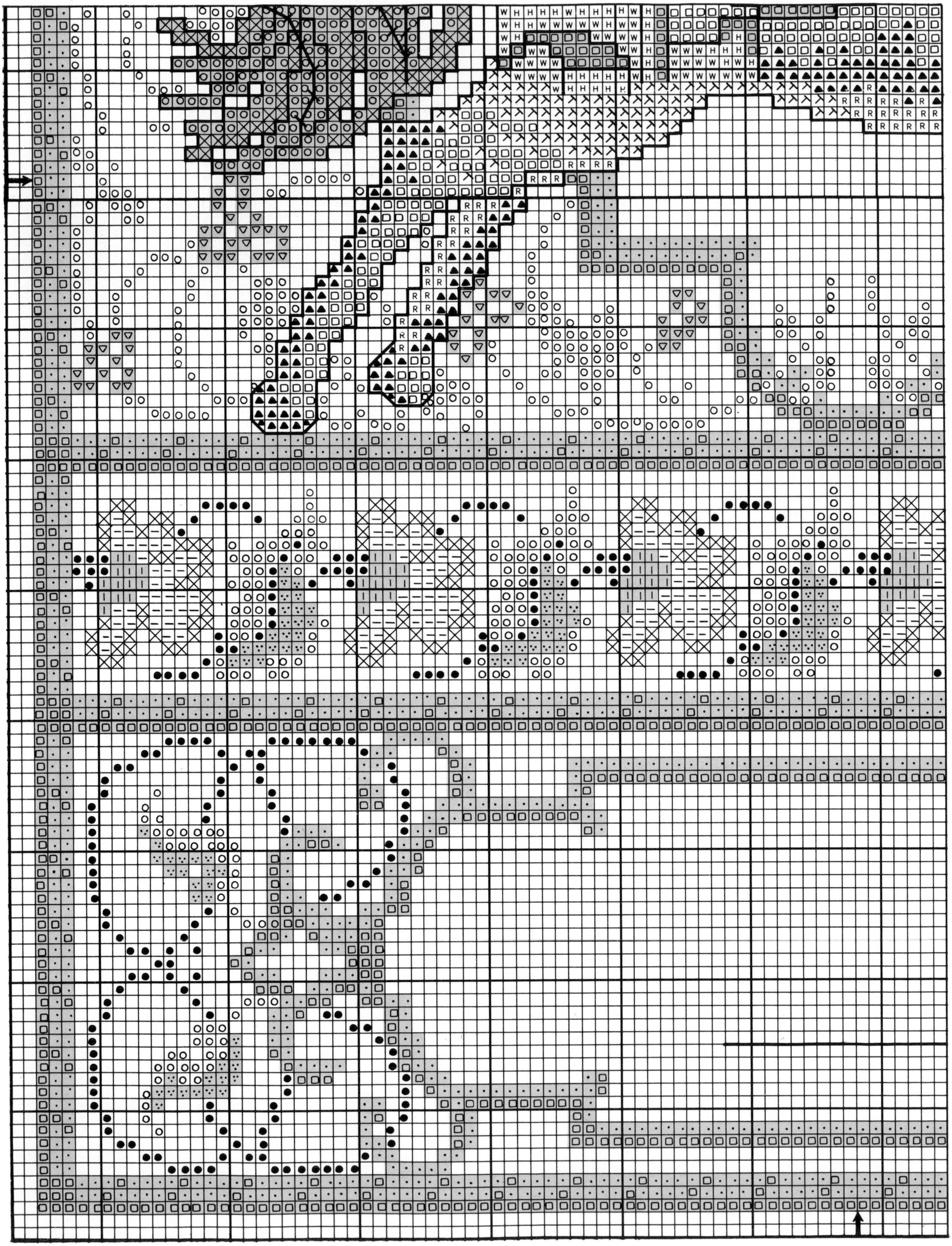

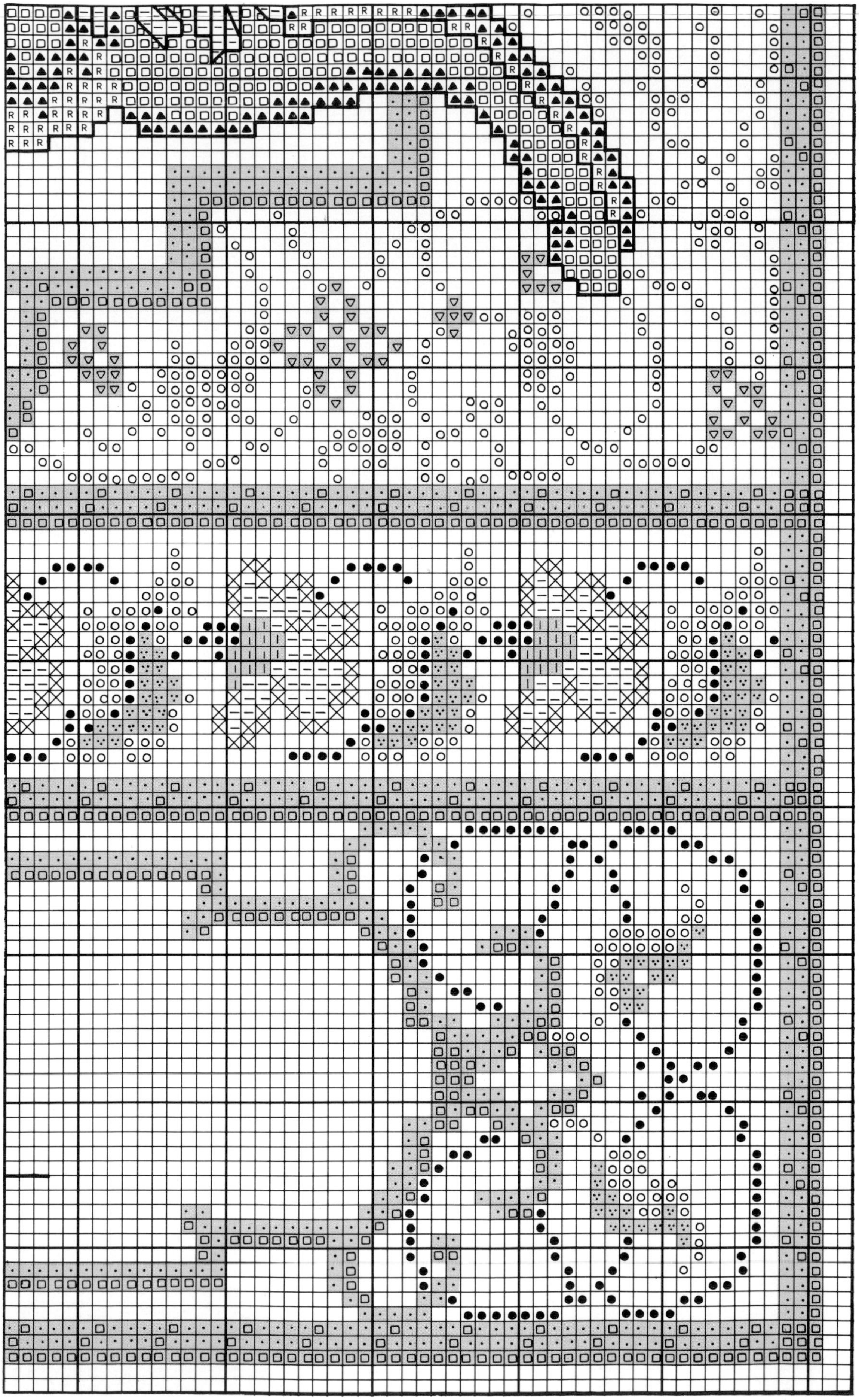

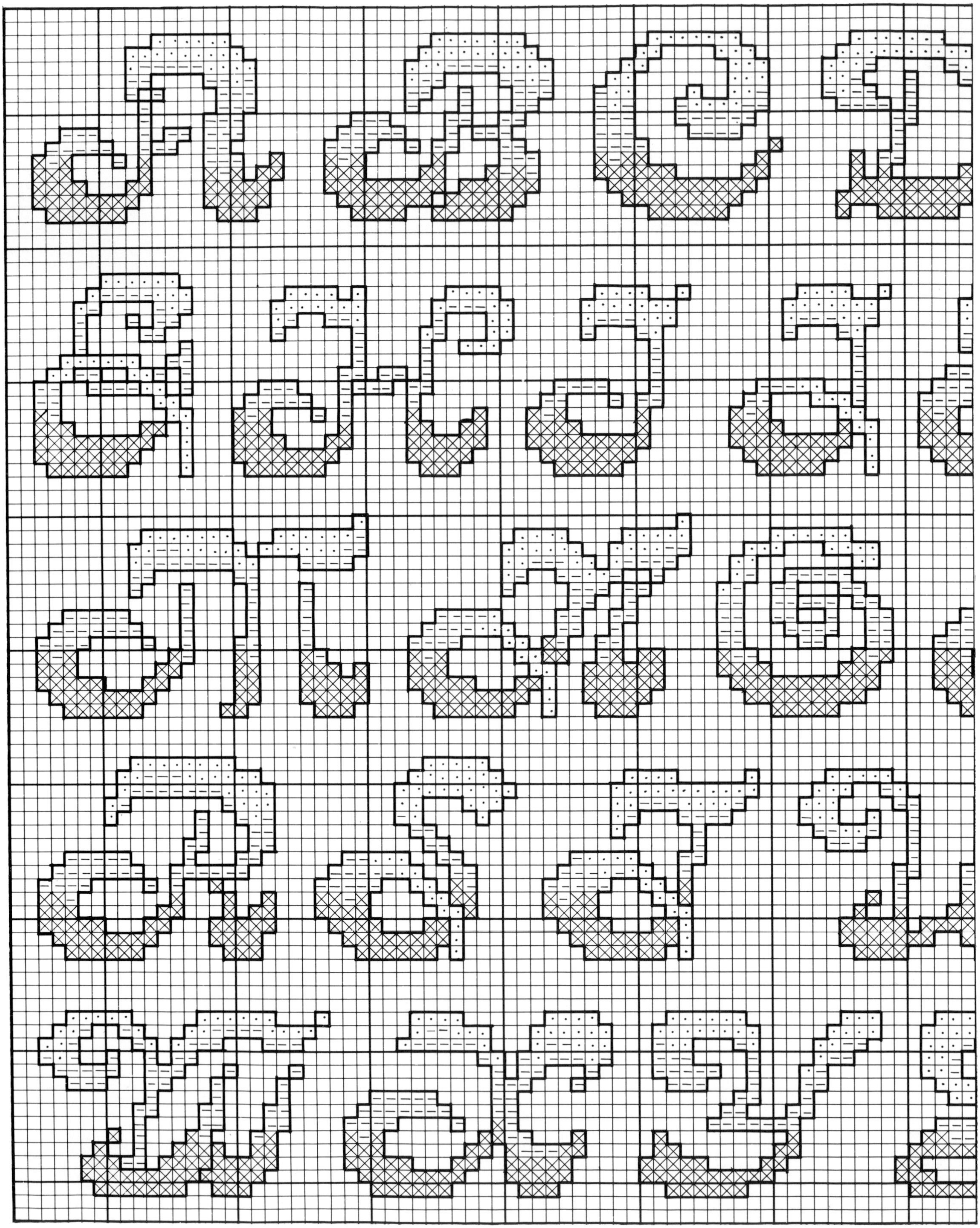

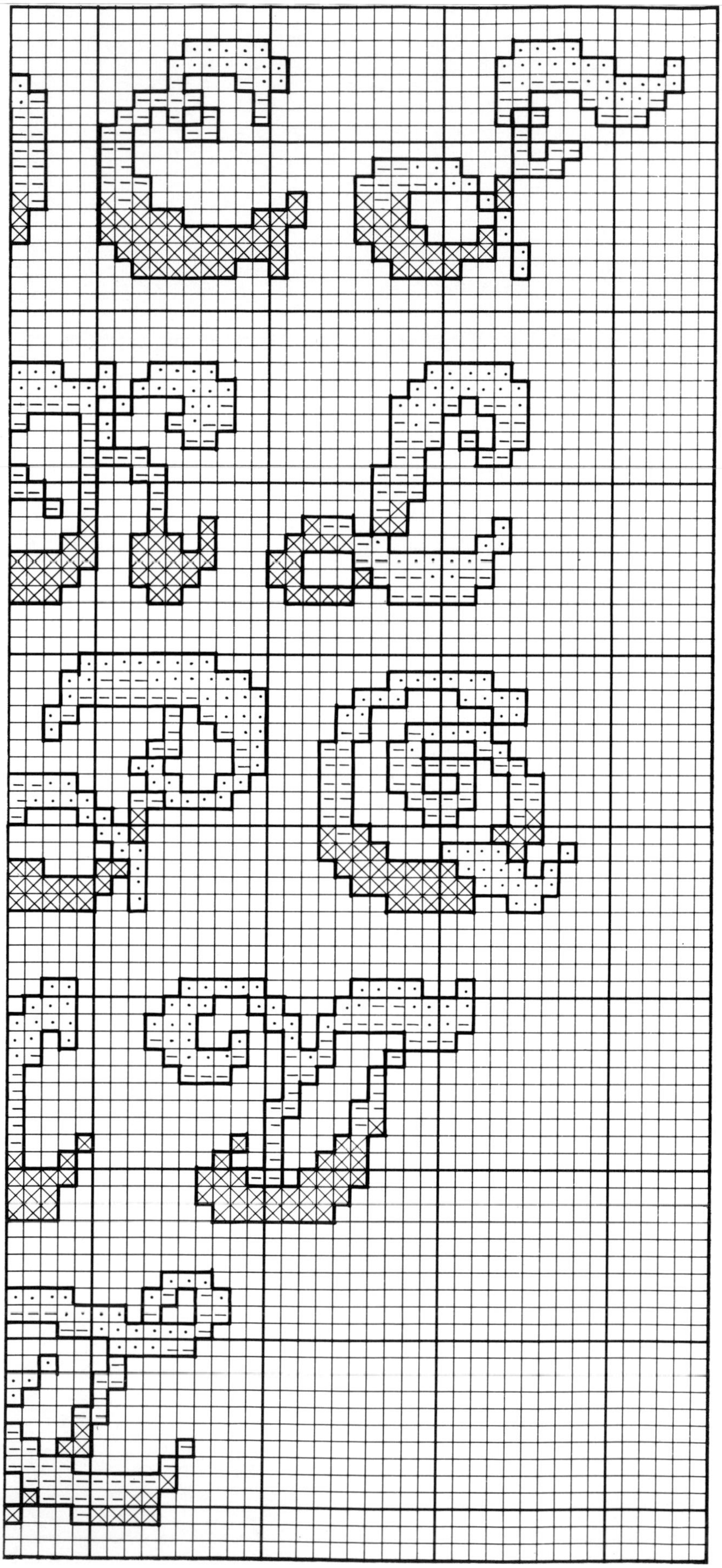

ABCDEFGHIJKLM

QUILT BLOCKS

Quilt blocks stitched in crosses are something you might question,
but, in our quest for quasi-quilts, it's only a suggestion.
They're very quaint, quick to stitch, with a quality guarantee.
Now, isn't that enough excuse to form a quasi-quilting bee?

Stitch Count: 75 × 112

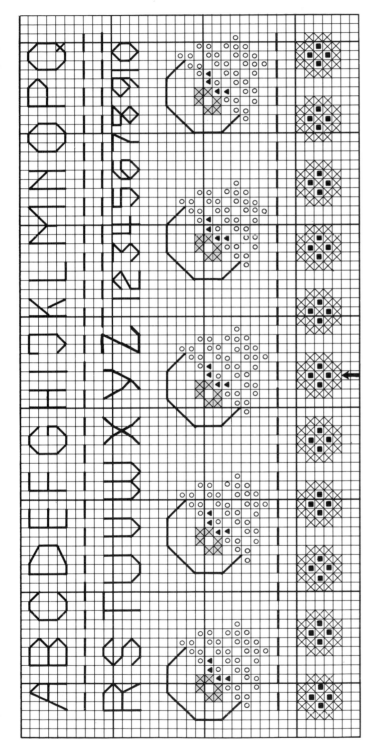

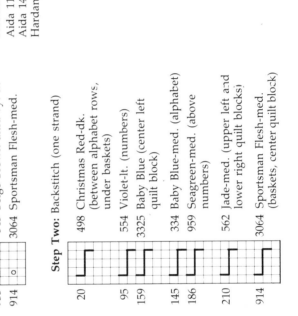

Stitched on black Aida 18 over one thread, the finished design size is 4⅛" × 6¼". The fabric was cut 10" × 12".

		FABRICS	DESIGN SIZES
		Aida 11	6⅞" × 10⅛"
		Aida 14	5⅜" × 8"
		Hardanger 22	3⅜" × 5⅛"

ANCHOR   DMC (used for sample)

Step One: Cross-stitch (two strands)

886	□	677	Old Gold-vy. lt.
8	–	761	Salmon-lt.
74	+	3354	Dusty Rose-lt.
44	✕	814	Garnet-dk.
95	▬	554	Violet-lt.
99	▪	552	Violet-dk.
159	·	3325	Baby Blue
145	✕	334	Baby Blue-med.
149	∴	311	Navy Blue-med.
187	●	958	Seagreen-dk.
208	□	563	Jade-lt.
210	△	562	Jade-med.
212	▲	561	Jade-vy. dk.

933	○	543	Beige Brown-ultra vy. lt.
914	○	3064	Sportsman Flesh-med.

Step Two: Backstitch (one strand)

20		498	Christmas Red-dk. (between alphabet rows, under baskets)
95		554	Violet-lt. (numbers)
159		3325	Baby Blue (center left quilt block)
145		334	Baby Blue-med. (alphabet)
186		959	Seagreen-med. (above numbers)
210		562	Jade-med. (upper left and lower right quilt blocks)
914		3064	Sportsman Flesh-med. (baskets, center quilt block)

ABCDEFGHIJKLM

REFLECTION OF THE SUN

It is very rare in nature
to recapture a reflection
of the sun reaching down
to reform such perfection.
I guess the real reason
I reminisce about that ray,
is that it renewed my faith
on that remarkable day.

Stitch Count: **142 × 122**

Stitched on light brown Linen 25* over two threads, the finished design size is 11⅜″ × 9¾″. The fabric was cut 18″ × 16″. (See Suppliers for flower thread, beads and Jaceron.)

* Use fabric with this stitch count only.

FLOWER THREAD (used for sample)

Step One: Cross-stitch (one strand)

- ■ 720 Beige Brown-med.

Step Two: Beadwork

- ∴ Cream (MPR 123T)
- ✕ Pale Peach (MPR 148T)
- F Ice Green (MPR 561T)
- △ Antique Silver (MPR 556T)
- □ Bronze (MPR 221T)
- ● Copper (MPR 330K)

Step Three: Chain Stitch (see Diagram)

- A 700 Beige Brown-lt.
- B 720 Beige Brown-med.
- C 715 Beige Brown-dk.

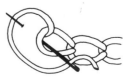

Diagram: Chain Stitch

Step Four: Couching

| ▲ | #7 | Silver Jaceron (pearl purl) |

Step Five: Strands of Beads

Cream (MPR 123T)
Pale Peach (MPR 148T)
Ice Green (MPR 561T)
Antique Silver (MPR 556T)
Bronze (MPR 221T)

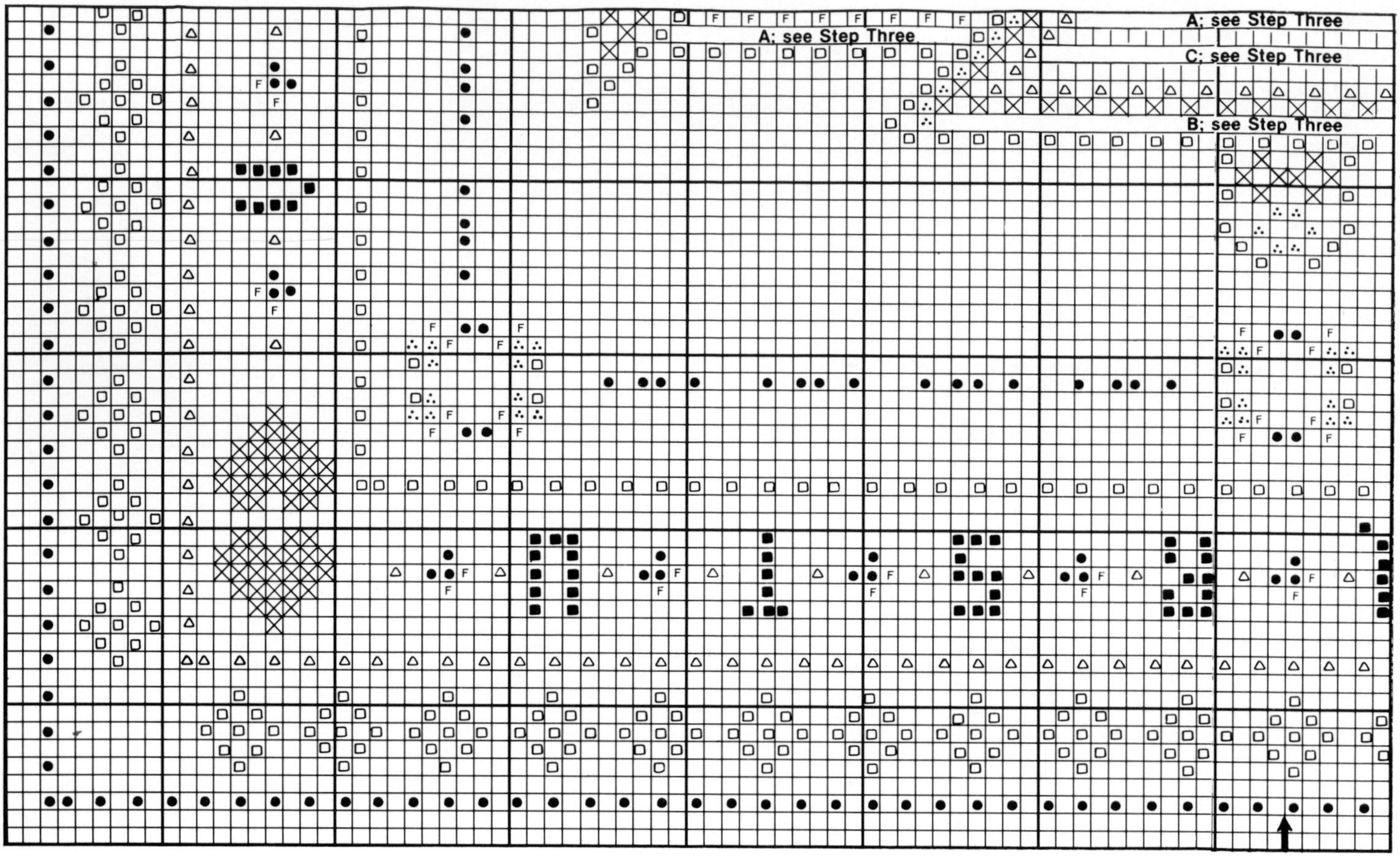
A; see Step Three
A; see Step Three
C; see Step Three
B; see Step Three

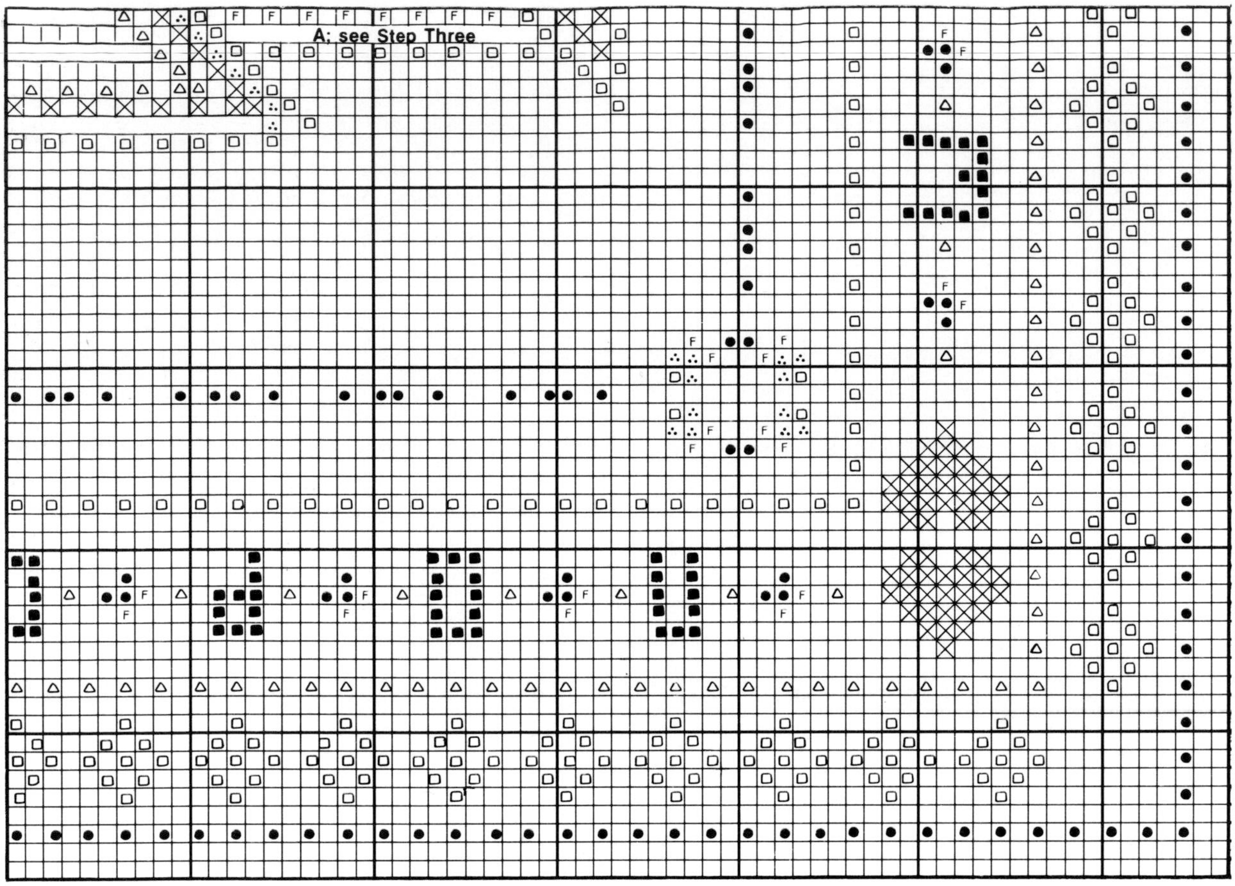
A; see Step Three

ABCDEFGHIJKLM

SWEET SIXTEEN

Sally Smith went to sleep
and dreamed about the scene
when on the sixth of September,
she'd be sweet sixteen.
At this Saturday social,
her first smooch would be had;
but what surprised her the most
is it wasn't all that bad!

Stitch Count: **103 × 90**

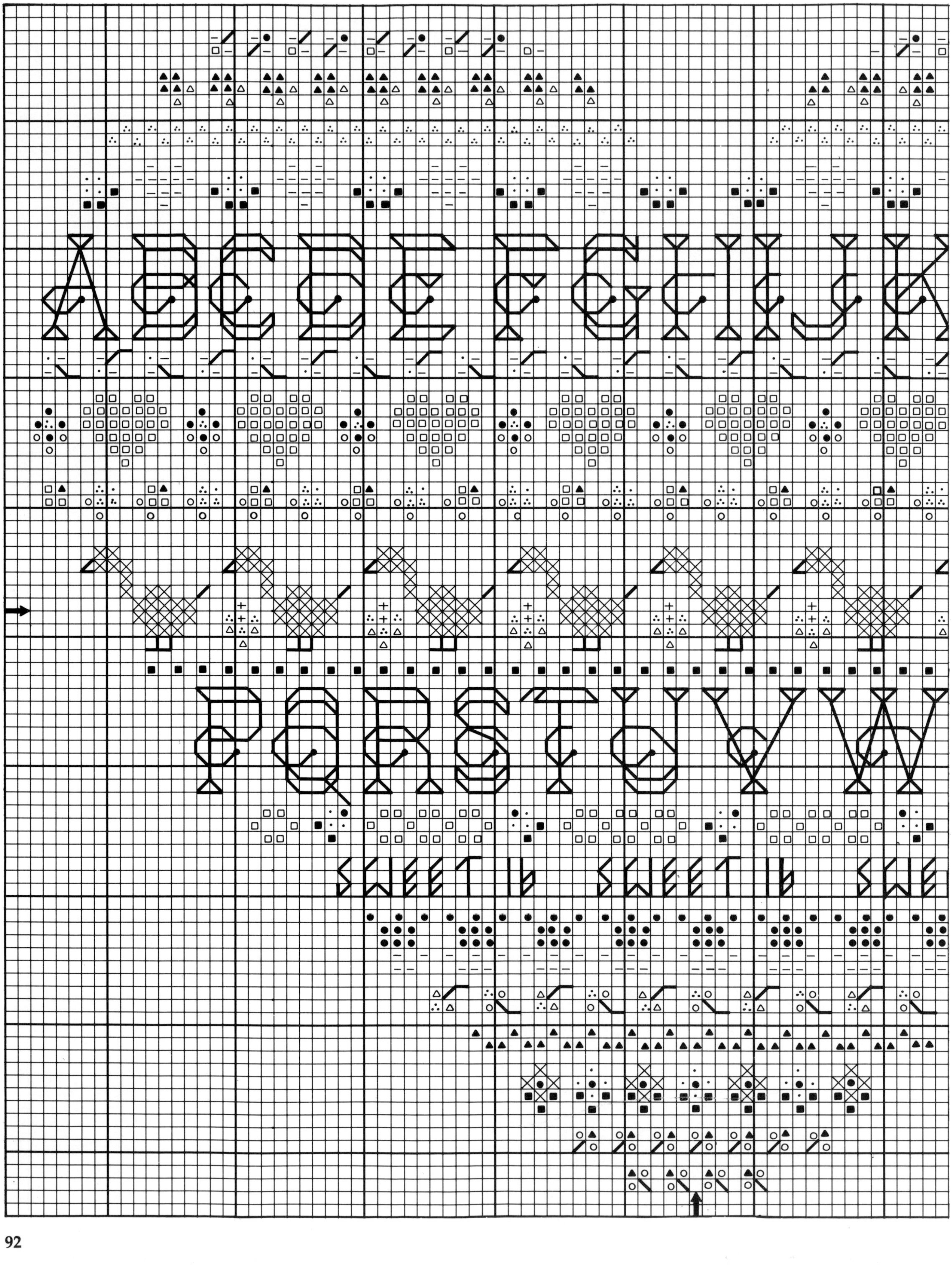

ABCDEFGHIJK

PQRSTUVW

SWEET 1b SWEET 1b SWE

92

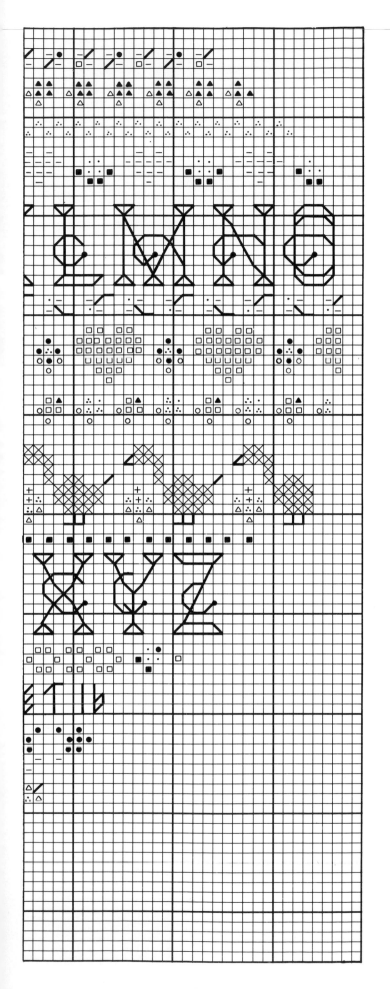

Stitched on cream Belfast Linen 32 over two threads, the finished design size is 6½" × 5⅝". The fabric was cut 13" × 12".

ANCHOR   DMC (used for sample)

Step One: Cross-stitch (two strands)

ANCHOR		DMC	
886	X	677	Old Gold-vy. lt.
24	·	776	Pink-med.
66	●	3688	Mauve-med.
95	∴	554	Violet-lt.
117	□	341	Blue Violet-lt.
118	▲	340	Blue Violet-med.
213	−	369	Pistachio Green-vy. lt.
214	△	368	Pistachio Green-lt.
215	○	320	Pistachio Green-med.
876	■	502	Blue Green
900	+	928	Slate Green-lt.

Step Two: Backstitch (one strand)

66		3688	Mauve-med. (geese)
118		340	Blue Violet-med. (lettering)
213		369	Pistachio Green-vy. lt. (stems — to match leaves)
214		368	Pistachio Green-lt. (stems — to match leaves)
215		320	Pistachio Green-med. (stems — to match leaves)

Step Three: French Knots (one strand)

118	●	340	Blue Violet-med.

FABRICS   **DESIGN SIZES**
Aida 11   9⅜" × 8⅛"
Aida 14   7⅜" × 6⅜"
Aida 18   5¾" × 5"
Hardanger 22   4⅝" × 4⅛"

TODAY AND TOMORROW

I think I'll move mountains
'round two o'clock today;
three thousand troops strong
can't get into my way.
Tomorrow I'll treat you
to clouds in formation,
but the third day I think
I'll take a vacation.

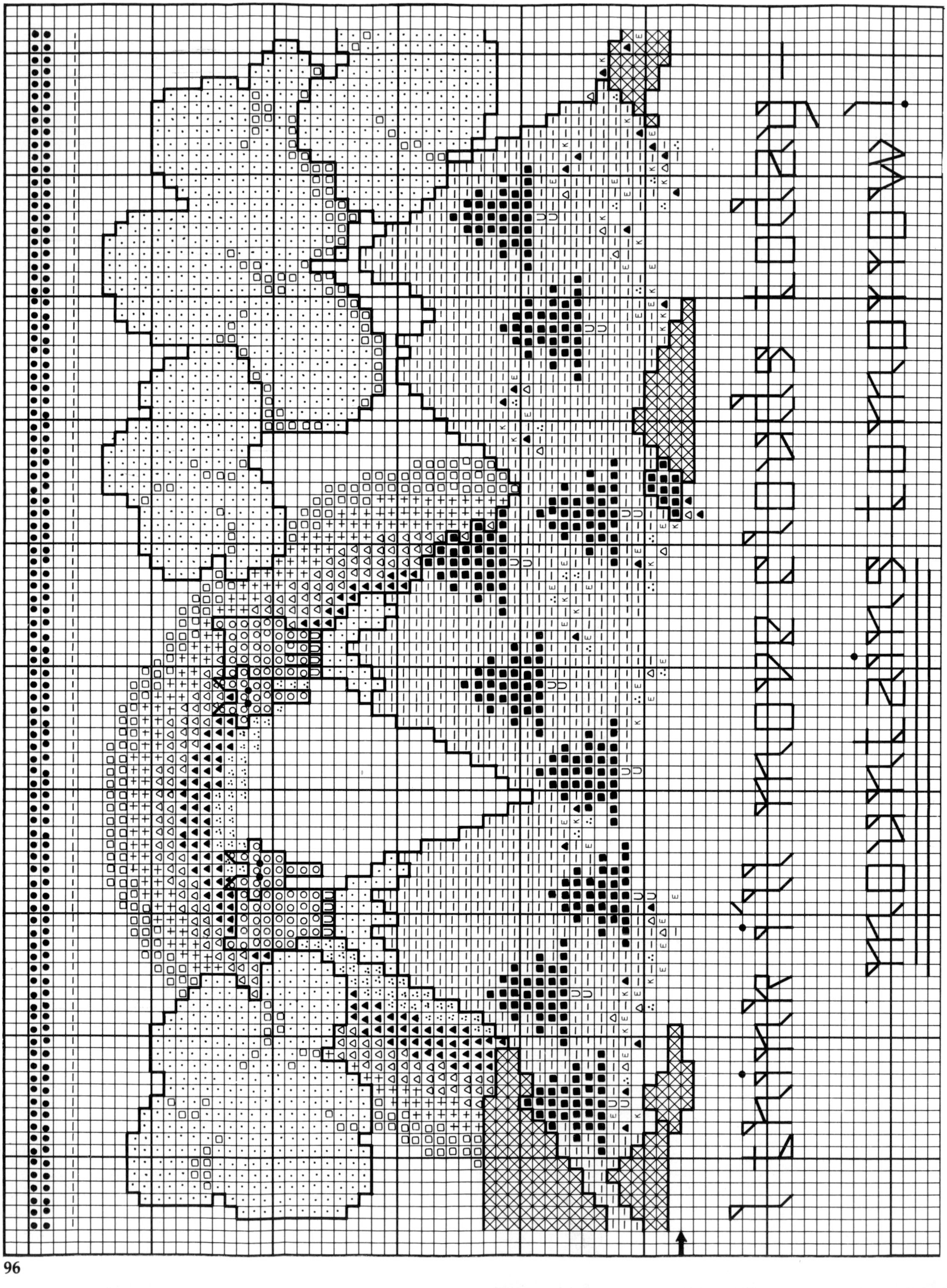

Stitch Count: 98 × 106

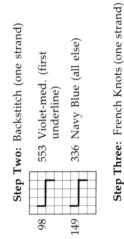

Stitched on white Linda 27 over two threads, the finished design size is 7¼″ × 7⅞″. The fabric was cut 14″ × 14″.

ANCHOR   DMC (used for sample)

Step One: Cross-stitch (two strands)

1	·		White
386	○	⌀	746 Off White
295	∴	⚎	726 Topaz-lt.
304	◢	◣	741 Tangerine-med.
26	△	◿	957 Geranium-pale
76	ᴋ		603 Cranberry
47	ᴇ		321 Christmas Red
108	+		211 Lavender-lt.
98	—		553 Violet-med.
159	▫		827 Blue-vy. lt.
256	✕		704 Chartreuse-bright
246	▪		986 Forest Green-vy. dk.
149	●		336 Navy Blue
905	⊔		3031 Mocha Brown-vy. dk.

Step Two: Backstitch (one strand)

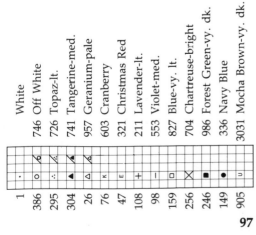

98	553 Violet-med. (first underline)
149	336 Navy Blue (all else)

Step Three: French Knots (one strand)

149	336 Navy Blue

FABRICS   **DESIGN SIZES**

Aida 11	8⅞″ × 9⅝″
Aida 14	7″ × 7⅝″
Aida 18	5⅛″ × 5⅞″
Hardanger 22	4½″ × 4⅞″

ABCDEFGHIJKLM

UNTIL WE MEET AGAIN

Your looks remain unbeaten and your kisses are unmatchable,
I well may be uncertain but it seems like you're uncatchable.
If I'm unwed this time next year I'll go utterly insane;
so, consider this an ultimatum for when we meet again.

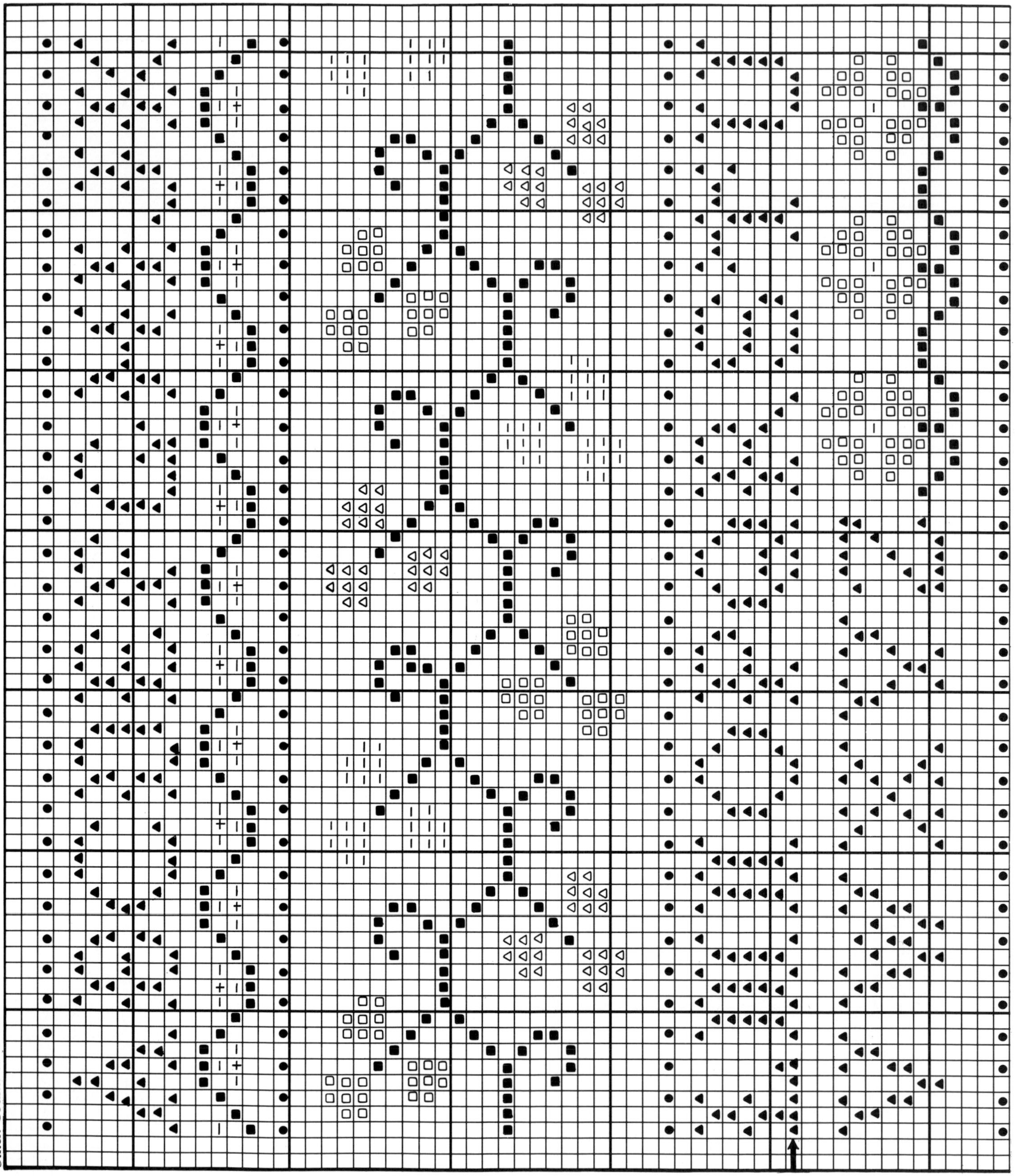

Stitch Count: 69 × 95

Stitched on cream Aida 14 over one thread, the finished design size is 4⅞" × 6¾". The fabric was cut 11" × 13". (See Suppliers for beads.)

ANCHOR   DMC (used for sample)

Step One: Cross-stitch (two strands)

886	o ⊘	677 Old Gold-vy. lt.
8	—	353 Peach Flesh
868	◁	758 Terra-Cotta-lt.
882	▲	407 Sportsman Flesh-dk.
893	□	224 Shell Pink-lt.
167	· ∕	598 Turquoise-lt.
264	∴	772 Pine Green-lt.

843	·	3364 Pine Green
876	●	502 Blue Green

Step Two: Backstitch (one strand)

876	502 Blue Green

Step Three: Beadwork

+	Yellow (MPR 128T)

FABRICS   **DESIGN SIZES**

Aida 11	6¼" × 8⅝"
Aida 18	3⅞" × 5¼"
Hardanger 22	3⅛" × 4⅜"

ABCDEFGHIJKLM

VICTORIAN INVITATION

Let's invite the Vanderbilts, the Vincents and Van Dykes,
the Viscount and viceroyalty, surely you know the likes.
Don't forget the villagers. . .how our wedding guests increase. . .
virtually everyone will come, so this adding now must cease!

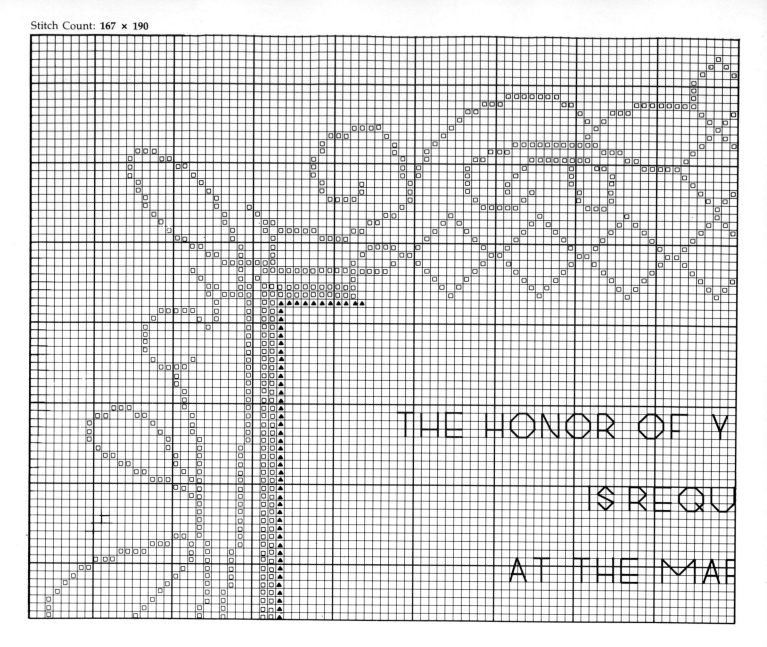

THE HONOR OF Y

IS REQU

AT THE MAF

Stitched on driftwood Belfast Linen 32 over two threads, the finished design size is 10½″ × 11⅞″. The fabric was cut 17″ × 18″.

ANCHOR   **DMC** (used for sample)

Step One: Cross-stitch (two strands)

| 392 | ▢ | 642 Beige Gray-dk. |
| 903 | ▲ | 640 Beige Gray-vy. dk. |

Step Two: Backstitch (one strand)

| 903 | ⌐ | 640 Beige Gray-vy. dk. |

Step Three: French Knots (one strand)

| 903 | ● | 640 Beige Gray-vy. dk. |

FABRICS   **DESIGN SIZES**
Aida 11   15⅛″ × 17¼″
Aida 14   11⅞″ × 13⅝″
Aida 18   9¼″ × 10⅝″
Hardanger 22   7⅝″ × 8⅝″

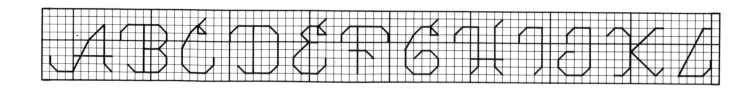

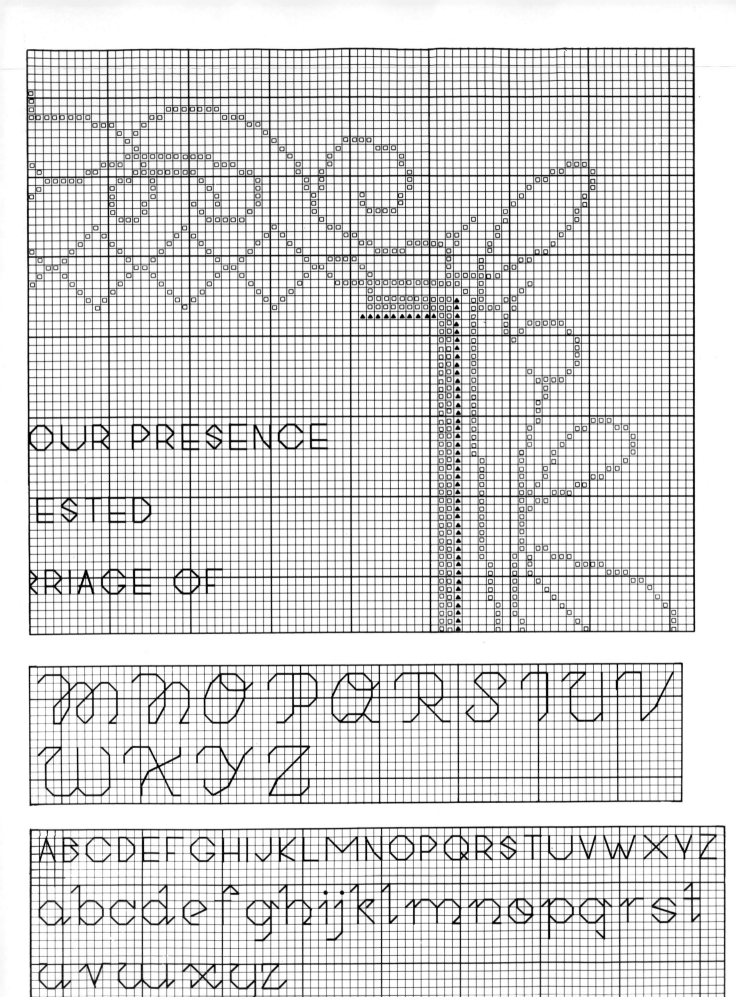

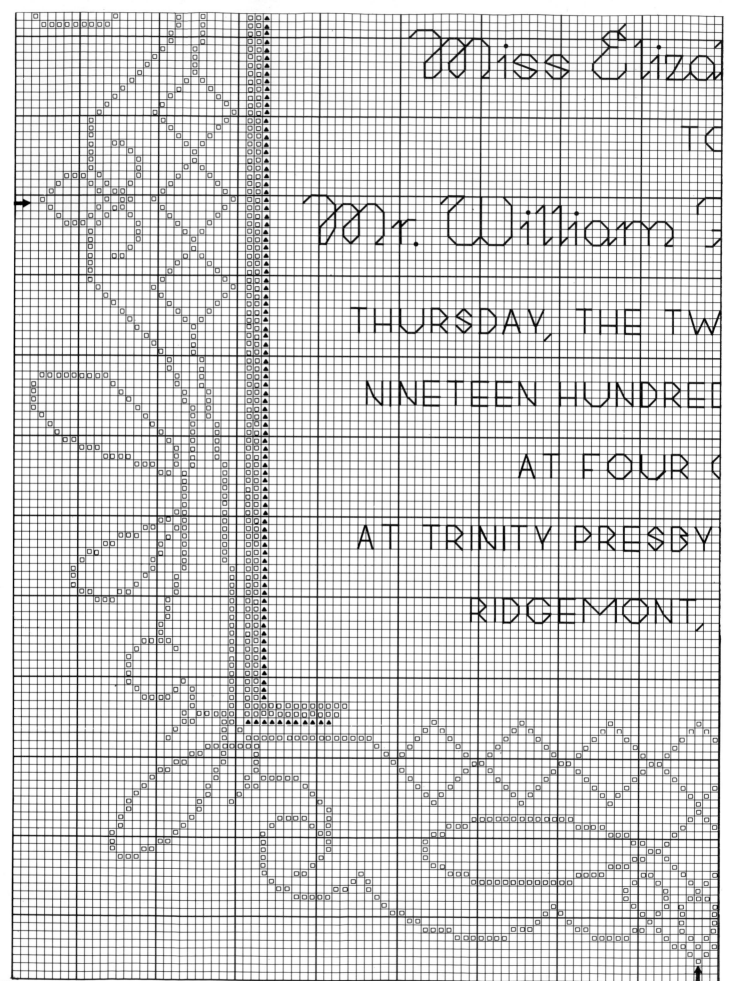

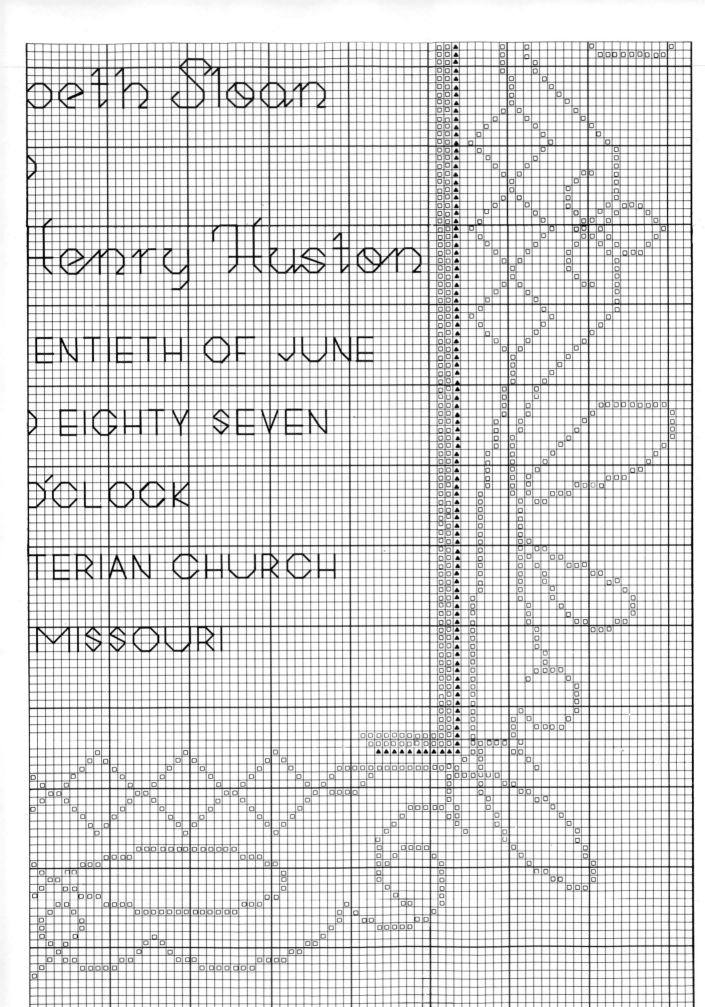

oeth Sloan

enry Huston

ENTIETH OF JUNE

EIGHTY SEVEN

O'CLOCK

TERIAN CHURCH

MISSOURI

ABCDEFGHIJKLM

WELCOME

You made this for our wedding gift; we hung it on our wall;
wherever we've moved it was always up to welcome one and all.
We've watched our visitors come and go, from all states east to west;
but wonder why you haven't come; you'd be an honored guest!

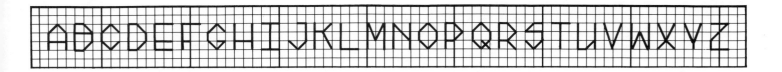

Stitched on cream Belfast Linen 32 over two threads, the finished design size is 4½″ × 5¾″. The fabric was cut 11″ × 12″. To cross-stitch a name, transfer letters to graph paper. Mark centers of graph and begin stitching in the center of space indicated for personalizing.

Kloster blocks and wrapping:
Each grid line on the graph represents two threads of linen. A Kloster block is five satin stitches worked over four threads. Stitch with #8 Pearl Cotton. Complete all Kloster blocks.

Cut threads from area to be worked; note blank areas on graph. Using #8 Pearl Cotton, weave over first two threads and under two; continue until bar is full.

ANCHOR	DMC (used for sample)

Step One: Cross-stitch (two strands)

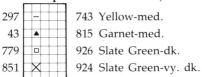

297	–	743 Yellow-med.
43	▲	815 Garnet-med.
779	□	926 Slate Green-dk.
851	✕	924 Slate Green-vy. dk.

Step Two: Backstitch (two strands)

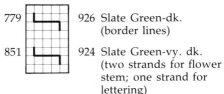

| 779 | | 926 Slate Green-dk. (border lines) |
| 851 | | 924 Slate Green-vy. dk. (two strands for flower stem; one strand for lettering) |

Step Three: Kloster Blocks and Wrapping (one strand)

| 43 | | 815 Garnet-med. #8 Pearl Cotton |

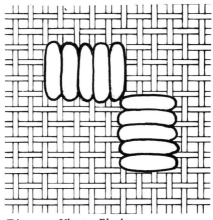

Diagram: Kloster Blocks

FABRICS	DESIGN SIZES
Aida 11	6½″ × 8¼″
Aida 14	5⅛″ × 6½″
Aida 18	4″ × 5″
Hardanger 22	3¼″ × 4⅛″

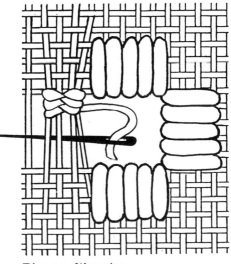

Diagram: Wrapping

EXTRA-SPECIAL

Excuse me, but this sampler
really needs no explanation;
to say you're extra-special
is no exaggeration.
You're an excellent example
of a friend who's always true;
which explains exactly why
I stitched this piece for you.

Stitch Count: **149 × 41**

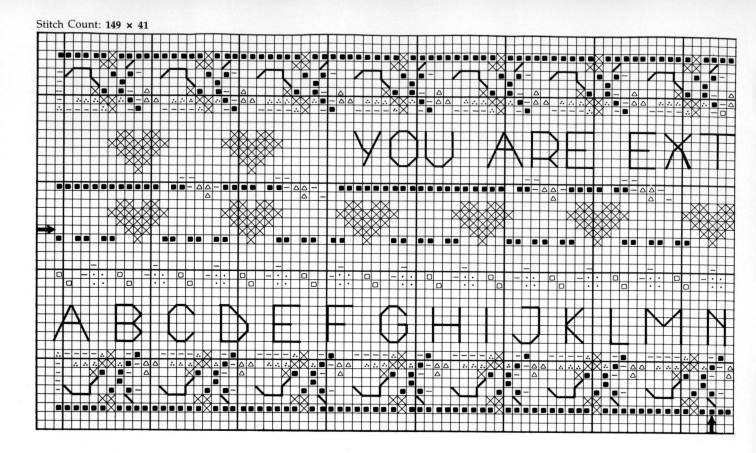

Stitched on white Belfast Linen 32 over two threads, the finished design size is 9¼″ × 2½″. The fabric was cut 16″ × 9″.

ANCHOR   **DMC** (used for sample)

Step One: Cross-stitch (two strands)

886	−	677 Old Gold-vy. lt.
893	✕	224 Shell Pink-lt.
159	△	3325 Baby Blue
920	∴	932 Antique Blue-lt.
213	·	369 Pistachio Green-vy. lt.
214	■	368 Pistachio Green-lt.

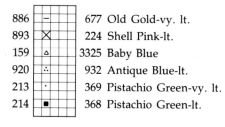

Step Two: Backstitch (one strand)

| 920 | | 932 Antique Blue-lt. (lettering) |
| 214 | | 368 Pistachio Green-lt. (flower stems) |

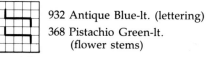

Step Three: Beadwork

| □ | Pink (MPR 145T) |

FABRICS	**DESIGN SIZES**
Aida 11	13½″ × 3¾″
Aida 14	10⅝″ × 2⅞″
Aida 18	8¼″ × 2¼″
Hardanger 22	6¾″ × 1⅞″

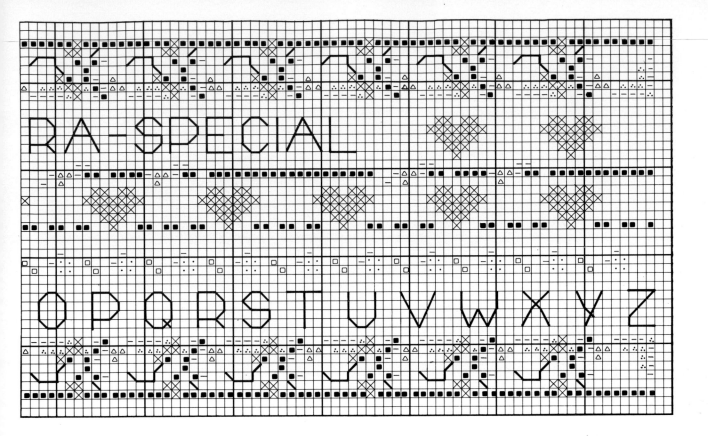

RA-SPECIAL

OPQRSTUVWXYZ

115

ABCDEFGHIJKLM

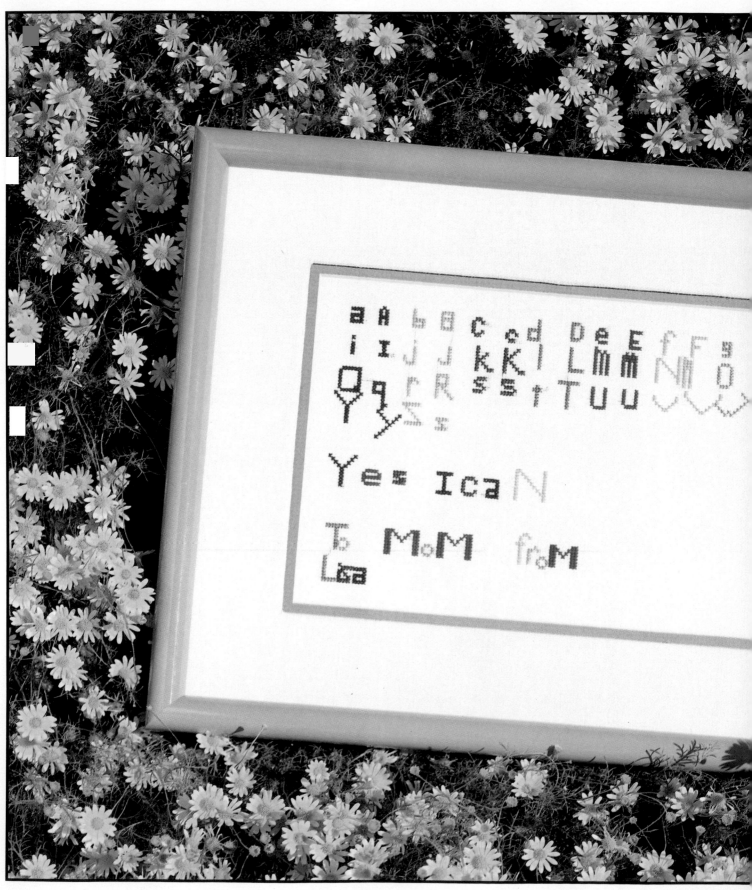

YES, I CAN

When I was very young,
I surprised my mommy Terrece
with this design "Yes, I Can,"
my childhood masterpiece.
I used some yellow, red, and blue;
she said, "It looks great!"
but now that I'm experienced
just wait 'till I turn eight!

Stitch Count: **160 × 88**

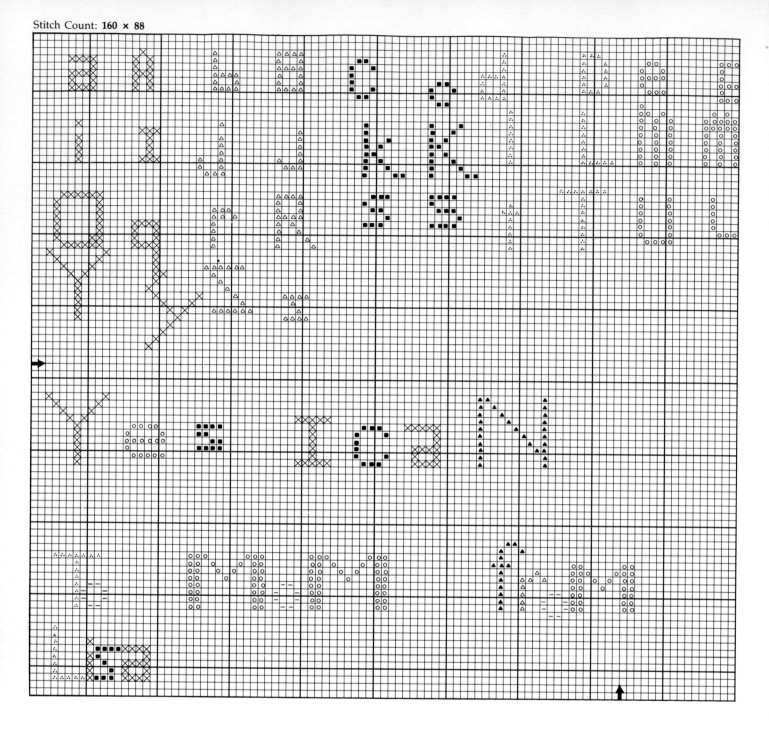

Stitched on white Belfast Linen 32 over two threads, the finished design size is 10″ × 5½″. The fabric was cut 16″ × 12″.

FABRICS	DESIGN SIZES
Aida 11	14½″ × 8″
Aida 14	11⅜″ × 6¼″
Aida 18	8⅞″ × 4⅞″
Hardanger 22	7¼″ × 4″

ANCHOR   DMC (used for sample)

   Step One: Cross-stitch (two strands)

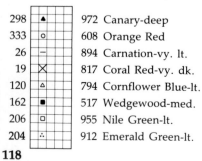

298	▲	972	Canary-deep
333	o	608	Orange Red
26	–	894	Carnation-vy. lt.
19	✕	817	Coral Red-vy. dk.
120	△	794	Cornflower Blue-lt.
162	■	517	Wedgewood-med.
206	▢	955	Nile Green-lt.
204	∴	912	Emerald Green-lt.

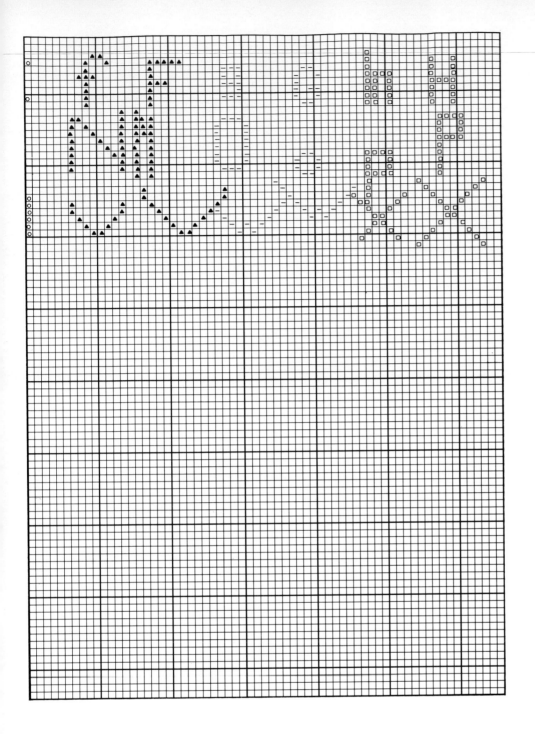

ZIPPETY-DO-DAH

Don't zip past this piece
because it's last in our book;
it's brimful of zest
and worth a long look.
There are zillions of parties
being thrown every day,
and this zany piece
adds a zippety-eh!

Stitched on white Linda 27 over two threads, the finished design size is 9⅛" × 11⅜". The fabric was cut 16" × 18".

ANCHOR			DMC (used for sample)
Step One: Cross-stitch (two strands)			
1			White
387			712 Cream
293			727 Topaz-vy. lt.
881			945 Sportsman Flesh
881			945 Sportsman Flesh (one strand)
316			740 Tangerine
48			818 Baby Pink
24			776 Pink-med.
42			309 Rose-deep
108			211 Lavender-lt.
105			209 Lavender-dk.
158			747 Sky Blue-vy. lt.
167			519 Sky Blue
121			793 Cornflower Blue-med.
149			311 Navy Blue-med.
203			954 Nile Green
186			993 Aquamarine-lt.
189			991 Aquamarine-dk.
942			738 Tan-vy. lt.
362			437 Tan-lt.
914			3064 Sportsman Flesh-med.
380			839 Beige Brown-dk.
903			640 Beige Gray-vy. dk.
8581			647 Beaver Gray-med.

Step Two: Backstitch (one strand)

42		309 Rose-deep (inside girl's dress)
167		519 Sky Blue (blue flower stems at bottom)
189		991 Aquamarine-dk. (rose flower stems, dotted line)
914		3064 Sportsman Flesh-med. (girl's bangs)
149		311 Navy Blue-med. (all else)

Step Three: French Knots (one strand)

42		309 Rose-deep
149		311 Navy Blue-med.

FABRICS	DESIGN SIZES
Aida 11	11⅛" × 13⅞"
Aida 14	8¾" × 10⅞"
Aida 18	6⅞" × 8½"
Hardanger 22	5⅝" × 7"

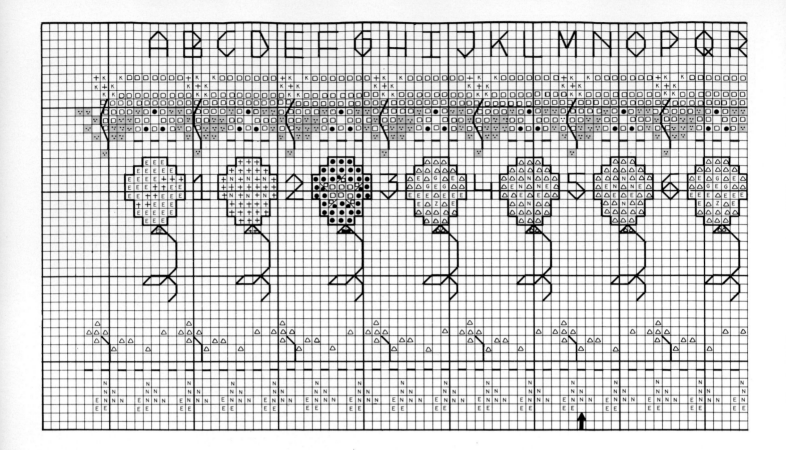

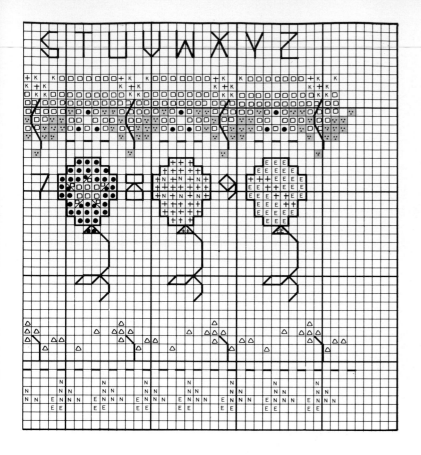

GENERAL INSTRUCTIONS

CROSS-STITCH

Fabrics: Most fabrics used in this book are even-weave fabrics made especially for cross-stitch and are available in needlework departments or shops. If you cannot find the fabrics in your area, refer to Suppliers. Fabrics used for the models in the photographs are identified in the sample information by color, name and thread count per inch.

Finished Design Size: To determine the finished size of a design, divide the stitch count by the threads per inch of the fabric. When designs are stitched over two threads, divide stitch count by half of the threads per inch.

Needles: Use a blunt tapestry needle that slips easily through the holes and does not pierce the fabric. With fabric that has eleven or fewer threads per inch, use needle size 24; with fourteen threads per inch, use needle size 24 or 26; with eighteen threads or more per inch, use needle size 26.

Preparing Fabric: Cut the fabric 3″ larger on all sides than the finished design size, or cut as indicated in sample information. To keep the fabric from fraying, whipstitch or machine-zigzag the raw edges.

Hoop or Frame: Select a hoop or stretcher bars large enough to hold the entire design. Place the screw or clamp of the hoop in a 10 o'clock position (or 2 o'clock, if you are left-handed) to keep from catching the thread.

Floss: Cut the floss into 18″ lengths. For best coverage, run the floss over a damp sponge and separate all six strands. Put back together the number of strands recommended for use in sample information. If the floss becomes twisted while stitching, drop the needle and allow the floss to unwind. The floss will cover best when lying flat.

Centering Design: Find the center of the fabric by folding it from top to bottom and again from left to right. Place a pin in the point of the fold to mark the center. Locate the center of the graph by following the vertical and horizontal arrows. Begin stitching at the center point of the graph and fabric. Each square on the graph represents a complete cross-stitch. Unless indicated otherwise in the sample information, each stitch is over one unit of thread.

Securing Floss: Never knot floss unless working on clothing. Hold 1″ of thread behind fabric and secure the thread with the first few stitches. To secure the thread when finishing, run it under four or more stitches on the back of the design.

Backstitching: Complete all cross-stitches before working backstitches or accent stitches. When backstitching, use the number of strands indicated in the code or one strand fewer than was used for cross-stitching.

Stitching Method: For a smooth stitch, use a "push and pull" method. Push the needle straight down and completely through the fabric before pulling it up.

Carrying Floss: Do not carry floss more than ½″ between stitched areas because the loose threads, especially dark ones, will show through the fabric. Run the floss under worked stitches on back when possible.

Cleaning Completed Work: After making sure fabric and floss are colorfast, briefly soak the completed work in cold water. If it is soiled, wash it gently in mild soap. Roll the work in a towel to remove excess water; do not wring. Place the work face down on a dry lightweight towel and press it with a warm iron until it is dry.

Personalizing: To cross-stitch an initial or name, transfer letters to graph paper. Mark centers of graph and begin stitching in center of space indicated for personalizing.

STITCHES

Cross-Stitch: Bring the needle and thread up at A, down at B, up at C, and down again at D (Diagram 1). For rows, stitch all the way across so that the floss is angled from the lower left to the upper right; then return (Diagram 2). All the stitches should lie in the same direction.

Diagram 1: Cross-Stitch

Diagram 2: Cross-Stitch Rows

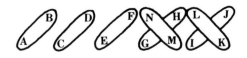

Half-Cross: Indicated on the graph by a slanted line with the color symbol beside it; make the longer stitch in the direction of the slanted line. The half-cross stitch actually fits three-fourths of the area (Diagram 3).

Diagram 3: Half Cross-Stitch

Bring the needle and thread up at A and down at B, up at C and down at D. In cases where the two colors meet, the graph will indicate how the colors make up the completed stitch (Diagram 4).

Diagram 4: Half Cross-Stitch

Bring the needle and thread up at A and down at B, up at C and down at D. In cases where the two colors meet, the graph will indicate how the colors make up the completed stitch (Diagram 4).

Backstitch: Work from left to right with one strand of floss (unless indicated otherwise in the code). Bring needle and thread up at A, down at B, and up at C. Going back down again at A, continue in this manner (Diagram 5).

Diagram 5: Backstitch

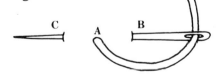

Diagram 6: French Knot

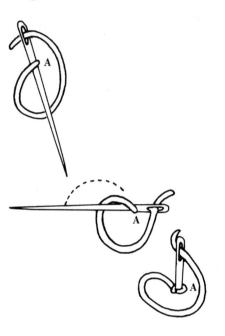

BEADWORK
With one strand of embroidery floss, attach beads to fabric with a half-cross, lower left to upper right. Secure the beads by returning the thread through the beads, lower right to upper left. Complete an entire row of half-crosses before returning to secure all the beads. See Suppliers for the source of beads used for the projects throughout the book.

SUPPLIERS

All products are available retail from Shepherd's Bush, 220 24th Street, Ogden, UT 84401; (801) 399-4546; or for a merchant near you, write the following suppliers:

Zwiegart Fabrics—Zwiegart® / Joan Toggitt Ltd., 35 Fairfield Place, West Caldwell, NJ 07006

Zwiegart Fabrics used:

   White Aida 14
   Cream Aida 14
   Light Blue Aida 14
   White Aida 11
   Black Aida 18
   Rustico 14
   Black Hardanger 22
   White Linda 27
   White Belfast Linen 32
   Cream Belfast Linen 32
   Driftwood Belfast Linen 32
   Terra-Cotta Lugana 25
   Mocha Dublin 25

Glenshee Linen 29 (natural)—Anne Powell Heirloom Stitchery, P.O. Box 3060, Stuart, FL 33495

Jobelan (white, cream)—Wichelt Imports, Inc., Rural Route 1, Stoddard, WI 54658

Beads—MPR Associates, P.O. Box 7343, High Point, NC 27264

Ribbon - C.M. Offray & Son, Route 24, Box 601, Chester, NJ 07930-0601

Flower Thread—Ginnie Thompson Guild, P.O. Box 465, Pawleys Island, SC 29585

Jaceron—Kreinik Manufacturing, P.O. Box 1966, Parkersburg, WV 26101

THE VANESSA-ANN COLLECTION

DESIGNERS

Trice Boerens
Linda Durbano
Vickie Everhart
Margaret Marti
Jo Packham
Tina Richards
Julie Truman
Lisa Woodruff
Terrece Woodruff

STAFF

Jo Packham and
Terrece Beesley Woodruff, owners

Gloria Baur
Vicki Burke
Kristen Jarchow
Susan Jorgensen
Margaret Marti
Barbara Milburn
Pamela Randall
Julie Truman
Nancy Whitley

Our special thanks to these people for the use of their homes and businesses in the photography of this book: Clyde and Pat Buehler; Arnie and Nan Smith; Scott Buehler; Susan Whitelock; Ivywood, Ogden, Utah; Kaysville County Library, Kaysville, Utah; Shepherd's Bush, Ogden, Utah; Mary Gaskill at Trends and Traditions on Historic 25th Street, Ogden, Utah; Utah State University Extension Farm, Kaysville, Utah; and Washington School Inn, Park City, Utah.